INNOVATION
IN FIVE ACTS

SOURCEBOOK

INNOVATION IN FIVE ACTS

STRATEGIES FOR THEATRE AND PERFORMANCE

Edited by Caridad Svich

Theatre Communications Group
New York
2015

Innovation in Five Acts: Strategies for Theatre and Performance is published by Theatre Communications Group, Inc., 520 Eighth Avenue, 24th Floor, New York, NY 10018-4156

This publication is made possible in part by the New York State Council on the Arts with the support of Governor Andrew Cuomo and the New York State Legislature.

TCG books are exclusively distributed to the book trade by Consortium Book Sales and Distribution.

Library of Congress Cataloging-in-Publication Data
Innovation in five acts : strategies for theatre and performance / edited by Caridad Svich.
pages cm
ISBN 978-1-55936-511-6 (paperback)
ISBN 978-1-55936-840-7 (ebook)
1. Theater—Production and direction. I. Svich, Caridad, editor.
PN2053.I527   2015
792.02'3—dc23   2015016598

Cover and text design by Kitty Suen and Monet Cogbill

First TCG Edition, June 2015

CONTENTS

PROLOGUE

ACT ONE: FOCUS

ACT TWO: BEING WITH

ACT THREE: TASK

ACT FOUR: AT PLAY

ACT FIVE: LET'S

EPILOGUE

AT PLAY IN THE COMMONWEALTH
(A PROLOGUE)

Caridad Svich

I am humbled by the sheer abundance of passion, talent, skill, rage, and artistry in this, our field. This collection—these five acts—which you hold in your hand or touch on the screen of your reading device—began as a blog series I curated for the 2013 Theatre Communications Group National Conference and its Artistic Innovation arc. The series yielded over seventy essays and reflections, which then bled into the curating process of the 2014 series I curated for the 2014 TCG Conference on Crossing Borders, which, in turn, yielded over eighty articles. Clearly, this is no 'dry spell' in our vibrant, intergenerational, cross-disciplinary communities engaged in the practice and theory of theatre and performance. Instead what I have been witnessing, not only through these two curated salons, but also in the wider work I do as an artivist, is that there is an increased desire to articulate the passions and processes and questions that go into art-making and its production, be they from the administrative or artistic side. Coupled with this passion to articulate is also one devoted to perhaps a healthy skepticism around articulation itself—a desire too to dis-articulate and just 'do.' Both stances are tied, I believe, to how practitioners observe the effects and after-effects of the modish, instantaneous and sometimes facile articulation of ideas on social media.

Sometimes it does feel as if perhaps one is trying to navigate a bizarre maze of what is deemed 'expressivity' to actually locate profound, reflective, rigorous thought expressed in essay, article or other modalities in our networked world. Yet, the creative optimist in me—the one who makes art and works in culture in various aspects—also believes that sometimes one of the great pleasures to be found in our field—the one to which we tend to on a daily basis with our lives and our existent and non-existent bank accounts, too—is when the talk turns to inspiration, and inspiration to awakened thought. The arts, after all, the making of art pieces are, at day's end, about how to re-see the world, re-imagine it and transform it somehow. In this collection, revised from the blog series, for this publication, the move from inspiration to awakening occurs frequently, and at times, almost as if by chance. The writers who have contributed their work to this volume, after all, were not aware of what the others were writing. Yet, how is it that connections, sometimes ecumenical in spirit and sometimes contentious, across disciplines, modes of practice, and perspectives on the nature of art-making are forged? I do not think it is mere serendipity, but rather something to do with the word "innovation" in and of itself.

When I was first asked to curate the blog series for TCG Circle moderated by August Schulenburg, who offers his remarks as the epilogue to this book-'play' in five acts, and he said that one of the central arcs of the 2013 TCG National Conference held in Dallas, Texas would be "artistic innovation," I was both delighted and a bit wary. After all, the word "innovation" is used to talk about fiscal ventures, car design, twitter chats and much more. In short, it is an overused word, and especially at conferences where the word can ring a hollow and perfunctory note as a catch-all term to "jazz up" the conversation. Everyone wants to feel at some level that what they are doing and how they are doing it is innovative. In the United States, in particular, there is a historical impetus toward creating the 'next big thing' in the 'next new way.' Cultural primacy is often rewarded to what carries with it the mere whiff of innovation. My wariness was warranted, in other words.

As curator, a part of me felt that the title and ostensible topic of the arc was loaded and could lead to potentially threadbare and rather cursory and even flippant takes on the subject to ones that might find themselves weighted down by the history of the word in not only culture-at-large but also within the field itself. But what I was surprised to discover, as the series unfolded bit by bit and practitioners, scholars and administrators shared their written reflections, was how unguarded, despite sharing similar healthily skeptical reactions to the word and topic itself, and generous the responses were—how devoid, in other words, of snark and bitterness. With good humor, intelligence, thoughtfulness, rigor and wit, author after author offered their considered take on the subject, unlocking new perspectives, unearthing old ones, and in general, doing what artists do best when they are walking on ground they trust and among colleagues who are not sitting before them in continual and sometimes stultifying judgment—and that is, open our eyes, hearts and minds again.

In this edited collection, more than forty practitioners and scholars voice their whimsical, fiery, deeply impassioned, political, funny, sometimes elegiac and stinging words prompted by a call to write about "artistic innovation." Most of the artists write about innovations in form, or reactions to and against late capitalism and how its economic structures have made the deceptively simple impulse to say "Let's"—as Julie Felise Dubiner eloquently writes in her essay of the same name—a torturous and somewhat long-winded affair that has left many an idea for the making and production of art on the cutting room floor. This same impulse is echoed in Zac Kline's essay, which brims with the potential of the word "Yes"—how, in effect, a serendipitously thunderstruck moment of awe and wonder can occur when seeing work that makes you believe again in theatre's power. This same "Yes" is reiterated in Octavio Solis' essay on how innovative writing can make an audience and fellow practitioner become re-awakened to seeing the world anew. What's interesting, of course, is that this should be the goal each and every time, as hard as it may be: to make something because you want to have others see the world as if it were a new thing—new and wondrous, as Mark Schultz reminds us in his essay that centers on Shakespeare's *The Tempest*, and how the efficacies of wonder in art, or shall we say, the many uses of enchantment, reconnect us to the past, even as we are moving irrevocably forward.

This collection is divided into five acts, titled as follows: Focus, Being With, Task, At Play and Let's. As the titles suggest, each act or chapter looks at the overarching topic of artistic innovation from a particular perspective or energy field. The first act generally concentrates on how practitioners and scholars regard their work and the work of others, how they "pull focus," to quote writer/performer Jeff McMahon, and also how they handle the twinning strands of entrepreneurship—or what is sometimes referred to as part of the practical and administrative business of making art—and spiritual and aesthetic concerns.

The second act explores what it is like to "be with" art from the point of view of process and cross-cultural artistic exchange and acts of mentorship. In effect, what does art do, and "what can it do," to quote Andy Smith. In second acts of plays, by what tend to be deemed "conventional" standards, the real struggles of characters begin. It's where the beating heart of the drama kicks in. If this is so, then perhaps one way to consider the act/chapter as it is assembled here is to look at how the practitioners, scholars and critics represented here choose to face the necessity of art "being with" and not "at" fellow artists and students in a room, an audience, a neighborhood and larger aspects of society.

The third act centers on tasks to one degree or another, taking into account, of course, that "focus" and "being with" are part of the ongoing considerations of making and sharing work with others. Some of the tasks represented here are as simple as reading and viewing work. Octavio Solis reflects on key authors and productions of their work that have shaped the way he thinks about art-making. John Moletress analyses the violence of creation and its effects on process. Oliver Mayer looks at aspects of translation, code-switching and how speech acts affect the reception and perception too of written and produced works for live performance. But as a whole, the act places the "task at hand" and how it is dealt with or discovered in the room of play at its emotional center.

In the fourth act, putting work in motion, at play, is explored from multiple perspectives from oblique and direct angles. What does it mean exactly when you put something into play? How do bodies behave in motion with other bodies in a performance space? What struggles and intimacies of engagement are revealed when doing and showing play? These are some of the questions teased out in this act, which gathers together artists based in Berlin, London, Los Angeles, Minneapolis, and New York. They bring to this eclectic, wide-ranging metaphorical table a range of experiences in the field— from community-created work to classically-inspired material to movement theatre. Each offers their own singular perspective on the evolution of the craft, its hand-made qualities, and the essential nature of what it means to cross the stage: to walk in someone else's shoes, mark the space, and inscribe it with meaning, feeling and courage.

The fifth act, some scholars may argue, is when plays pull out all the stops, when everything either unravels or comes to a roaring conclusion somehow. Usually, there is a deus ex machina moment in the fifth act or perhaps some great battle is waged or an elaborate wedding ensues. In others words, in the fifth act, things fall apart and civilization ends–the illusion and representation of civilized life as represented in the narrative–or things are restored to some degree of order or harmony. I have titled the fifth act "Let's," not only because that is the title of the final essay but because in thinking about how an event in space is made, an event that is often called a play, the desire to acknowledge that a temporary commonwealth has been built throughout the duration of the event, is central. We are all in this together. We will go out into the light together. Let's, you know, do something with what we have seen, learned and/or experienced. That's what happens in the fifth act, beyond any prescribed structural expectations. The journey of the event moves through the body of the audience and into the world, where every day, every waking moment, the invitation to do and make and transform and better society is possible. It is a hopeful, optimistic call to arms because art-making in and of itself, regardless of a specific work's subject matter, is optimistic, for it speaks in its very marrow, of the belief that the art and act of doing means something and can effect some measure of change.

Culturally, for about thirty years now in the US, we have been progressively steeped in wondrously fast and ever-upgrading innovations in digital technology, market-driven, consumer-aimed and otherwise. Twin engines of profit and wizardry have created a "boom" for faster, better, and seemingly wiser materials and objects: the latest app, the newest phone, the sleeker design, the more portable, functional, gigabyte heavy, efficient mega-machinery–all, hopefully, at our fingertips, and able to be cradled gently in our palms.

Theatre can never really compete with faster, "better" culture. Heather Woodbury and Lisa Schlesinger and others in this collection, argue that we look toward a slow, slower theatre instead. In other words, not to mimic what our culture is already doing faster and arguably "better" than us, but to counter it, and by so doing, do one of the central jobs of art, which is the job of resistance.

We live in a commonwealth. We live in a commons. We seek the greater good.

Theatre, at its best, at its most daring, confounding, and most vulnerable, does make us a better society.

As agents of change we have a responsibility not only to ourselves–individually and to each other–but to the greater good of the field: how to sustain it, nurture it, keep it moving forward without leaving its histories and elders behind, and how to cope with and make space for the unruly gardens of promise and potentiality that are new works for live performance, be they written by someone in their adolescence or someone in their 80s.

You see, that's the thing about art: the new stuff–the seeing the world through wondrous new eyes stuff–can happen anytime.

We only have to recall that story about a reader for an international theatre festival who was reading a new Caryl Churchill play, and being surprised when meeting her to discover that she was in her mid-70s. "But I thought you were in your 20s!" the reader is said to have remarked.

Why?

"Because the work...is so, so new."

Is it idealistic or quixotic to consider how we can build a more sustainable theatre ecology, one that fosters more spaces of non-industry–more spaces for dreaming and tinkering and trying things out and failing and failing again and failing some more–so that truly new work can be made?

If we believe that what we do matters, truly matters, in the grand scheme of things, in the spiritual sense of things, in how line and light and thought and motion and breath and skin and flight are theatre, rather than believe in or buy into a state of "reflexive impotence," a phrase coined by cultural theorist Mark Fisher in his book *Capitalist Realism* (2009)–a state that acknowledges the fact that things are bad, but nothing can be done about it except to carry on, or to quote the populist phrase "keep calm and carry on," wouldn't our theatres rise and keep rising, and keep expanding horizontally rather than vertically across the many gardens and backyards and humble lots and parks and makeshift platforms and altar spaces and spaces of remembrance and reflection too in this our ever widening field lit by an ever widening sky?

The score—the ever evolving, human score—is right before us, and it needs a little space for dreaming, and wrestling too through the passages in the heart and mind—known and unknown—that make this odd, strange, ephemeral thing called art happen.

If we allow ourselves to believe in more than the budget line and its hard, harsh realities and how it has come to dictate so many of our artistic decisions, and the ways we sometimes treat artists who for all intents and purposes, may just be seeking that crazy beautiful chaotic indefinable thing called "something new," and instead allow ourselves to re-believe as new disciples in the shape-shifting theatre church, in its sacredness and profanity combined, in its ability to move culture with sometimes just two actors, some light and some words in that moment, for those who are there, for those who were there once and are our ghosts now, will we then find and maintain the greater good?

I say: Yes! Let's.

Caridad Svich received the 2012 OBIE for Lifetime Achievement, the 2011 American Theatre Critics Association Primus Prize and has won the National Latino Playwriting Award sponsored by Arizona Theatre Company twice, including in the year 2013. Among her key works are *12 Ophelias, Iphigenia Crash Land Falls on the Neon Shell That Was Once Her Heart* and *The House of the Spirits* (based on the Isabel Allende novel). Two collections of her plays are published by Seagull Books and Eyecorner Press. She has also edited several books on theatre and performance for TCG, Manchester University Press, BackStage Books, and Smith & Kraus. She is alumna of New Dramatists, founder of NoPassport theatre alliance & press, and associate editor of *Contemporary Theatre Review* for Routledge, UK.

INNOVATION
IN FIVE ACTS

ACT ONE

FOCUS

INNOVATION IN 17
(WITH A KNOWING NOD TO BILL DRUMMOND)

Stephen Wrentmore

Theatre is a fluid, social art form that, as Hamlet would have it, "holds the mirror up to nature"; Heraclitus taught us that change is the only constant. A commitment to innovation seems like an inevitability in the arts and especially in theatre. But, change and innovation live in very different houses. In the rehearsal room we build from the script up... But, do we really innovate? Do we really change that much? Instead of writing an essay on innovation, here is a manifesto for thought.

The poised pen over the blank page

The "Yes" over the "It's difficult" (I knew that already)

Eyes of wonder and the audience gasp—like the child at Christmas

A playground of possibilities

Commit to knowing nothing, then deploy experience to tell a new story. Take those years of knowing nothing and combine them, mold them, discard them on the quest for something new worth knowing

Embrace failure as an inherent part of the creative process

Creativity lives beyond the stage in the very essence of your organizational being

Shared expertise trumps the single expert. Power to the collective "We"

> There is a (probably apocryphal) story of Kennedy visiting NASA in the early 60s He toured the facility asking people what they did. He came to the cleaner of the wash-rooms and asked the same question, "What do you do here?" To which the individual replied, "Sir, I'm helping to put a man on the moon."

Even if it's not true (and I hope it is) the point is:
What are your washroom attendants telling your customers about what you do?
What do they say about your art? Your organization? You?
Oh, and "We choose to go to the moon..." How high are your goals?

Be unique, distinctive and present. Commit to global ambition and inspiration, then invest in local connection. Why be generic when there are a myriad of local stories to be told and even more hungry ears to hear them? Leave ubiquity to the malls and the coffee shops

Start conversations with "What if" rather than "We used to" or "Historically"

Have you got 15 (20, 22, pick a number) years of experience? Or just one or two that you have repeated 15 times?

Abandon instrumentalist outcomes, worry less about what theatre does and worry more about what it is. Invest in the journey not the destination

Homogeny is boring and the antithesis of innovation, but the temptation is so strong. It is so easy to attempt recreation of someone else's hit rather than create your own

Education and Learning are not departments but a way of being

There is no ladder. There is barely a road map. If we invest in the new with the same vigor with which we cling to the past, what dreams may come?

Great art is successful because, in its moment, it speaks a truth that resonates. The rest is silence

Discuss.

Discuss.

Discuss.

Discuss.

You may say I'm a dreamer. But, I'm not the only one.

Stephen Wrentmore, originally from London and currently based in the USA, is a theatre director, arts consultant and teacher. He has worked in a diversity of countries, and was educated at Cambridge and the Royal Central School of Speech and Drama.

WHITHER INNOVATION?

Arthur Bartow

When I was a lad studying drama at the University of Oklahoma, theater seemed rife with innovation, largely because I knew so little about its history and everything was a revelation. At that time, academia was looking backward to the great experimenters of the early Twentieth Century, designers Gordon Craig and Robert Edmond Jones, playwrights Elmer Rice, Sophie Treadwell, and Eugene O'Neill. These innovators' experiments in symbolism and expressionism were efforts to summon the immaterial world, to stimulate an emotional and spiritual awakening within the medium of words, much the same as these movements had already impacted the visual arts. All of this was interesting, even exotic, but none of the results of their efforts seemed evident or even relevant to the professional theater we were seeing or what was being produced at school. We were locked into what we assumed was the truthful realism of the time, the bread and butter of commercial theatrical entertainment.

Arthur Miller, William Inge, William Saroyan, and Tennessee Williams were the best voices of the stage. Stanislavski's training methods for reaching into the actor's subconscious finally coincided with the new writing but had not yet been codified into university training programs. Our professors' own education sprang from an earlier age. Looking back, I think the oldest of our acting teachers was actually coaching the Delsarte method of bodily gestures and attitudes, an innovation in actor training imported from France in the previous century.

It had taken Lee Strasberg, Sanford Meisner, Stella Adler, and Robert Lewis a few decades of consistent training to insinuate Stanislavski's work into the popular culture through their own innovations to his techniques taught in private classes in New York. Most of their work was a result of the intense explorations by The Group Theatre during the 1930s. Twentieth-Century text required that actors be skilled at conveying coded meaning embedded within its dialogue. Shakespeare's elevated language supplied plot, subtext, and emotion, but modern audiences' ears were now accustomed to colloquial, less structurally complex speech. It would take such directors as Harold Clurman, Robert Lewis, and Elia Kazan to cement this new deeper naturalism to Twentieth Century theater and film. In the Midwest, we kept abreast of current trends through the monthly magazine, *Theater Arts*, the equivalent of today's *American Theatre*. Its articles were mostly about Broadway, although I do recall the magazine reporting a stir made by the Dallas Theatre Center's production of *Hamlet*. Artistic Director Paul Baker was using what he called cubist technique incorporating three actors to play different aspects of the melancholy Dane's psyche. There was also some news of the novel theatre-in-the-round created by Margo Jones (also in Dallas), which in turn had inspired replication by other women creating new theaters such as those by Zelda Fichandler in Washington DC and Nina Vance in Houston. None of us knew they were the vanguard of what was to blossom into the resident theater movement. These in-the-round theaters were often expanded with second spaces containing thrust stages, all resulting in bringing actors closer to their audiences. By removing the proscenium wall separating actors from the audience, a more intimate style of acting was required. These new theaters were also more cost efficient, often circumventing the need for heavy scenery. Sometimes innovation and savvy economics march hand in hand.

Innovation may also be confused with invention. Whereas invention refers to the creation of a seminal idea or method, innovation refers to how that idea or method may be extended, modified, and proliferated. Innovation usually surfaces from a network of inventions and for innovation to have a lasting impact not only is timing crucial but in order to establish itself audiences must be exposed to it over a consistent period of time.

The penetration of Stanislavski's actor training methods into mainstream theater brought forth opposition views from such artists and theorists as Bertolt Brecht and Jerzy Grotowski. While they were contrarians to Stanislavski's methods, their more distancing approaches were still in the service of bringing a deeper meaning to the theatrical experience. Not being as well documented and codified in their approaches and with fewer adherents than Stanislavski's followers, they filled a smaller niche in American theater. However, they contributed to the explosion of fervent experimentation during the 1960s.

Simultaneous to the resident theater movement, off-off Broadway theaters appeared and with them experimental theater artists. They included such iconic creators as Richard Foreman (Ontological Hysteric Theatre), Ruth Maleczeck, Lee Breuer, and JoAnne Akalaitis (Mabou Mines), Richard Schechner (The Performance Group), Elizabeth LeCompte (The Wooster Group), Robert Wilson, Charles Ludlam (The Ridiculous Theatrical Company), Joseph Chaikin (The Open Theater), Paul Zimet, Ellen Maddow, Tina Shepard (The Talking Band), and in Iowa Ric Zank (Iowa Theater Lab). They tested the boundaries of theatrical perception and were unique unto themselves usually scripting and designing their own productions. Many of these experimenters seemed uninterested in explaining themselves, in creating theories that could be replicated from their bodies of work. It was too intensely personal. It would take Mary Overlie, with her theory, The Viewpoints, to explain the process some of these creative artists had unconsciously been utilizing.

Choreographer Mary Overlie had been synthesizing a way to deconstruct the process of creating theater. She was inspired through participation in dancer/choreographer Merce Cunningham's experiments to deconstruct the language of movement and believed the same process could work to isolate the elements of dramatic construction. She boiled those elements down to six that she believed were universally incorporated by actors and directors to layer their work, and perhaps in this order of importance: story; emotion; timing; shape/design; movement; and space/blocking. She isolated these elements so that they could be developed separately and then reordered in any manner an artist might impose to bequeath an entirely new perspective. With this reordering of priorities, perhaps emotion or movement might take precedence over story, etc. This theory also borrowed of Structuralism, a method of criticism founded to deconstruct literary and philosophical texts and political institutions by the French academic, Jacques Derrida. Overlie's Viewpoints were then seized upon and expanded by teacher/artistic director Anne Bogart who amplified and popularized the idea of Viewpoints into her own process. She tested her innovations by creating an acting ensemble, the SITI Company, to riff on the original theory and apply the practical results to classical and contemporary works. These experiments have been widely disseminated to influence directors and actors.

In both of the examples of Stanislavski's and Overlie's inventions, a company of actors was essential to innovate and bring them into practical reality. For Lee Strasberg, inspired by Stanislavski, The Group Theatre was his vehicle, and for Anne Bogart her SITI Company. But it does take a village. The Group Theatre was lucky enough to have a playwright, Clifford Odets, emerge from the collective whose writing supported its efforts to take ensemble acting to new heights in America. Unfortunately for Viewpoints advocates, no playwright has yet emerged to fully utilize its tools. Bogart has expanded the original six viewpoints into myriad configurations lending further complexity to any work where they are applied. But they are most often employed in plays that were not necessarily conceived to welcome this process. No matter how innovative the director and designers may be, they are captive to the original intent of the written word. As was noted four hundred years ago, "The play's the thing." For innovations capable of such large influence to proliferate, all of the theatrical disciplines need to join in unison, writing, direction, acting, and design.

Theater is captive to its time but seems always to be playing catch-up to innovations in its sister arts, painting, literature, dance. The most successful examples of any period are when an innovation coincides with the inner life of its audience, freeing the viewers to access their feelings and thoughts. Regardless of the innovation, certain rules of the theatre seem to pertain no matter what new clothes are tailored to fit current trends. I'm most fond of the maxim expressed by Stanislavski's greatest pupil, the actor/director/teacher, Michael Chekhov. Chekhov thought that for a production to be successful actors as an ensemble must live together in the same world but also live in the same world as the play. It is possible for actors to be unified in their own style and still not be in the world of the writer. However, once all these worlds are in synch, it seems to work wonders on audiences. They relax and feel comfortable in joining that world. It is an instantaneous acceptance. This is an established observation, but sometimes rediscovering old truths can be as innovative as something fresh out of the box.

It is no accident that Americans cling to realism as their theatrical bread and butter. After 240 years we are still trying to understand who we are and to define our humanity. The director John Hirsch, whose family was taken away in a railway box car to Auschwitz and who knew better than most of us, said, "You have to learn to be human, and you have to keep relearning it." Perhaps this is the driving force behind the desire for innovation, to help each new generation rediscover its humanity.

We are now in the second or third generation of leadership in America's most significant theatrical innovation, the regional theatre movement. Without this delivery system, further innovation would be severely curtailed. These theaters are not always able to deliver new ideas but without a place for new waves of artistic leaders to practice speaking for their generation's perspectives on the world, the unarticulated needs of their community would be straightjacketed.

So how do we experiment, stumble our way toward progress, toward innovation during a time of economic deprivation? We must understand how essential creative inquiry is to our long-term survival. A friend employed by a New York department store was provided a risk budget each year. It had to be gambled on risky products or ideas. If it was not, she was held to account and had to defend herself. There was no expectation that the risky idea must succeed. If it failed, so be it, and if it succeeded, so much the better. Either result would help lead to the future. It was part of the corporation's process of understanding its community, its own capabilities, and its preparedness to grow creatively. Its Board understood and demanded this for its community and for its own survival.

Arthur Bartow was former Artistic Director, Drama Department, NYU's Tisch School of the Arts; Associate Director, Theatre Communications Group; Artistic Director, New Playwrights Theater, Washington DC and Theatre of the Riverside Church, New York. Publications include *The Director's Voice* and *Training of the American Actor.*

THEATRICAL INNOVATION: WHOSE JOB IT IS?

Howard Shalwitz

Innovation is a topic I've been thinking about for some time. Woolly Mammoth's founding manifesto, an embarrassing document I don't readily share, talks in somewhat grandiose terms about solving the contradiction between "the advance of theatre as an art form and the discovery of new and larger audiences" for theatre. I can't say we've achieved this goal, but I know we keep on trying. And for most of our 32-year history, our approach to innovation has been to support the development of the most provocative new American plays we can find, and to get them onto our stage with as much creativity as our talented company members and guest artists can muster.

But a new train of thought related to innovation started for me just two years ago at, of all places, the TCG conference in Chicago. For those who attended, I don't know if you had this experience, but toward the end of the conference I started to notice how many of the speakers had used the word "storytelling" at one point or other as a virtual synonym for the word "theatre." And I obsessed over this for a while, and began noticing in theatre brochures and websites how ubiquitous the words "story" and "storytelling" had become as descriptors for what we do. ("Great stories well told." "New stories that will touch your heart." Etc.) And this struck me as odd. When I was growing up, I thought of storytelling as something adults did with children at bedtime; whereas theatre, which I attended regularly from the age of ten, was quite different. It was about spectacle and language and music and magic and actors and emotions and ideas. We certainly wouldn't call Beckett a storyteller, and even to call Shakespeare a storyteller would be fairly reductive.

Now don't get me wrong—I'm not saying that stories aren't a critical part of what we do in the theatre, but to say they're the whole thing is a bit like a symphony orchestra saying they play melodies or an art museum saying they show pictures. So I started to wonder why this use of the word storytelling had become so widespread.

Just a few months before the Chicago conference I had taken my first trip to see theatre in Eastern Europe. I attended the Divine Comedy Festival in Krakow, which represents during a single week some of the best in Polish theatre from the previous year. And I can tell you, at that festival, there was hardly a story to be found! There was plenty of realism, and in fact, the level of physical and emotional detail from the actors was astonishing. And while there were certainly narrative elements, they were often secondary to the larger artistic **framing**—accomplished through installation-like scenic design or abstracted staging—which challenged the audience to look at the stories metaphorically or from unexpected angles. Texts were cobbled together or de-constructed from literary sources, films, classic plays, documentary material, community interviews, and improvisation. Even the one new play I saw that was actually scripted by a playwright, entitled NO MATTER HOW HARD WE TRIED by the brilliant young writer Dorata Maslowska, was only enough of a story to subvert the very idea of story.

At first it appeared to be a colorful portrait of a lower class Polish family as seen through the eyes of a teenage girl; then the lens shifted and it became clear that the characters were in a television show; and then the lens shifted again and it became clear that this family never existed because the character we thought was the grandmother had been annihilated as a young girl during the bombing of Poland in World War II. And the production, directed in visionary style by Grzegorz Jarzyna, had virtually none of the storytelling scenic elements we might imagine from reading the script, but just a few ratty pieces of furniture in front of a large video screen on which some of the images in the play were represented by childlike little squiggles, until the final scene when the bombing of Warsaw was depicted behind the grandmother and her non-existent granddaughter with overwhelming realistic force.

As you may have guessed, NO MATTER HOW HARD WE TRIED was one of the most powerful theatre experiences I've had in years. And what struck me was the way in which a very original playwriting idea worked in tandem with a highly unexpected directorial and design vision, and of course, with actors who really owned their roles, to create something that felt genuinely innovative.

At first I was tempted to dismiss the work I saw in Poland—and later in Bulgaria, Hungary, and Russia—by saying to myself that their tradition is more Brechtian while ours is Aristotelian, they have a director-driven culture while ours is playwright-driven, they get more government funding so they can rehearse longer and aren't so dependent on the box office, they sustain whole companies of artists while we have more of a freelance culture.

But the more work I saw, the more it became impossible not to be envious of a few things: first, that the variety of different kinds of work on their stages seemed wider; second, that it all felt like new theatre whether the script was new or old; third, that every play felt like an exuberant civic event because of the way the actors owned the material and seemed to be sharing it as an ensemble with the audience; and finally, that the audiences were noticeably younger than American audiences.

In the work I saw in Eastern & Central Europe, it sure looked as if the ideals of Woolly Mammoth's founding manifesto were being fulfilled: the art form was clearly advancing, and new audiences were being drawn in. How could I not get excited?

Shortly after my visit to Poland, three things happened in quick succession that made me start to question my own work at Woolly Mammoth.

First, I had lunch with Dominique Serrand, the great French-American director. I asked Dominique if he could characterize the difference between European and American directors, and he said something startling. "In Europe, the first job of the director is to re-invent the art form of theatre for every production. In the US, this job isn't even on the list of what most directors hope to achieve." And this crystallized what I had experienced in Europe: the feeling that there was a competition among different directors and companies to out-innovate one another, and this was their main way of attracting new audiences.

Was I encouraging directors to do this at Woolly Mammoth, I asked myself.

The second thing that happened was that I went through a series of planning meetings with members of Woolly Mammoth's acting company, including several award-winning actors who have worked at all of Washington's major theatres for two decades or more. When I asked how they would like to see our work evolve, they said they weren't looking for more roles, or better pay, though I'm sure they'd like that. What they said was that they were tired of showing up for the first day of rehearsal—at Woolly and every other theatre—and seeing the set and costume renderings for the first time, then rushing through a 4-week rehearsal process, sometimes absorbing continual script changes, feeling left out of the key decisions, and then having to go out on stage during the preview week feeling anxious and under-prepared because they didn't have time to investigate their roles.

And the third thing that happened: I attended the new play convening hosted by Arena Stage, entitled "From Scarcity to Abundance." During one of the sessions, three or four playwrights spoke about how helpful it is when theatres give them a great deal of control over the choice of their director and other collaborating artists, over casting, design, even the marketing language and images for their plays. And they used this word "control" several times. And so I raised my hand and said quite innocently that writers who give up a degree of control and make room for their collaborators to bring unexpected ideas to the table—these are the writers who, in my experience, actually get the best results, because they motivate everyone to contribute in original ways rather than constantly trying to second guess what's in the mind of the playwright.

In response, a couple of playwrights whose work I really admire explained with great passion how hard it is to struggle privately for many months to give birth to their words and dialogue, and then hand them over to directors and actors and designers for fear of what they'll do with them. And listening to this, I experienced an intense inner conflict: On the one hand, I was entirely sympathetic. I've devoted most of my career to supporting and empowering playwrights, and given the brevity of our rehearsal periods in the United States and the importance of premiere productions, it's little wonder that some of them want to control as many factors as they can. And on the other hand, as both an actor and director myself, I thought, couldn't actors say the same thing about how hard it is to wrestle with their text and build their characters, and having to submit themselves every day to the feedback of playwrights and directors? And couldn't directors and designers talk about their struggles to find a creative vision to lift up the play, but having to compromise to suit the needs of playwrights and actors?

Now, let me say, I know full well that no two playwrights are alike and many are highly collaborative. And frankly, I wouldn't have mentioned this isolated exchange if it weren't for the fact that, in the break after the session, two or three artistic directors came up to me and practically whispered how relieved they were that I had said something, implying that I had put my finger on one of the well-kept secrets in the field. And I started puzzling over what this secret is and how to express it, so bear with me, and I'll probably overstate this: The secret, I think, has nothing to do with whether playwrights are controlling; some are, some aren't, and the same could be said for actors, directors, designers, or for that matter, Artistic Directors. The secret may be that we've built an entire play-producing ecology in the resident theatres—supported by unspoken rules of engagement, backed up by agents, unions, contracts, schedules, and budgets—that places the entire burden for innovation at the feet of our playwrights, but asks little of directors, designers, and actors other than to try to fulfill the playwright's vision in the **same compressed rehearsal periods** we've had for years.

As a result, we don't often see productions like NO MATTER HOW HARD WE TRIED where innovative writing, directing, design, and acting all work together, adding layers of richness and complexity on top of each other. It takes too much time, requires too much exploration and experimentation on the part of the whole company. Whether we don't think those extra layers are necessary or we can't afford them, the result is the same. What we see on our resident stages is mostly new stories, because that's what we can accomplish with the tools we've given ourselves. They may be interesting or creative or important stories, they may be beautifully designed, but how often do we see the wider range of innovation, encompassing all the elements of theatre in a re-invention of the art form, which is the goal of companies in Europe and elsewhere?

As an Artistic Director whose job is to provide the proper resources for our artists, I asked myself: am I supporting playwriting innovations, but essentially **limiting** the potential of our actors, directors, and designers? What is this doing, in turn, to the innovative potential of our **playwrights**? Is this approach still galvanizing our **audiences**? Will it galvanize our **future** audiences?

While I was pondering these questions, I was lucky enough to have lunch with Zelda Fichandler, and she happened to refer to THE FERVENT YEARS as one of the most inspiring books about American theatre, and so I went back and re-read it. As most of you know, THE FERVENT YEARS is Harold Clurman's brilliant history of The Group Theatre in relation to the politics of the 1930s. It describes the foment of that period in New York, in the midst of the depression, with the rise of fascism in Europe and Communism in the US, and the urge that theatre artists felt to address these intense things going on around them.

Inspired by the Moscow Art Theatre, Clurman, along with Lee Strasburg and Cheryl Crawford, invited a group of about 25 actors, directors, designers, and playwrights to spend the summer of 1931 at a camp-like retreat in Connecticut, where they talked about theatre and politics, discussed the purpose of having a company, worked on exercises and plays, and considered what they might produce together. Returning to New York for the theatre season, they produced a few plays; and this basic pattern of summer retreats, and then two or three productions per season continued for most of the tumultuous life of The Group Theatre, which lasted only ten years.

I think that most theatre historians would agree that The Group— which launched the careers of Clurman, Strasberg, Clifford Odets, Stella Adler, Elia Kazan, Sanford Meisner, Lee J. Cobb, and many others—was, despite its short life, the most **revolutionary** theatre company in American history. It permanently transformed our ideas about the very purpose of theatre, about all the disciplines including acting, directing, playwriting, and design, and it laid the foundations for the core language about theatre, derived from Stanislavsky, that still dominates our pedagogy and our professional practice today. It also attracted whole new audiences to Broadway for plays that wouldn't have been considered financially viable before.

So here was yet another example, an American example, of advancing the art form and galvanizing audiences. And it had something in common with the work I'd seen in Europe: the innovations didn't come primarily from individuals, but from groups of artists working together, with advances in one discipline tied to advances in all the others.

American audiences still get excited when they see innovations in all the elements of theatre together. We've seen this in a few recent British imports to the US: BLACK WATCH, SLEEP NO MORE, and WARHORSE. All of these tell stories, but they are woven into a tapestry of innovative design, performance, and choreography.

There was one more thing I discovered in THE FERVENT YEARS that I think is a key for understanding innovation, and it's something that links all the examples above, from Europe, England, and the US. I want to call it: a shared sense of purpose. The members of The Group passionately wanted to reflect on stage the experiences of everyday Americans struggling at a moment in history. They wanted to ask questions, raise awareness, provoke debate.

Every good playwright has a deep sense of inner, private purpose. But when that purpose is taken up and shared by an ensemble of other artists, and through them with the audience, then it becomes something powerful, something public, and in some cases, something innovative.

So how can we think about innovation in practical terms? I'd like to share a simple paradigm shift that's starting to help me. But first I need to spend a few moments talking about the assembly line—and I'm sure you all know what I mean. Every theatre, certainly every resident theatre with its own performing space, needs an assembly line, and at Woolly Mammoth we've worked very hard to build one up over many years. It's a disciplined process to ensure that every play, in a fairly continuous stream of plays, will be ready for opening night. And the assembly line has three big steps:

For each production, we spend roughly **two years** doing what I'd like to call, step one, script search and development. If it's a new play, this includes a couple of workshops or readings to support the writer's process. If it's a recent New York or regional play, we inquire about the rights and learn it's being held up for a possible Broadway opening, and then a year or two later they finally release the rights and say it was never really going to Broadway in the first place. Even Shakespeare companies have their own version of this search and development process. "It's finally time to do Henry VIII, but how to make it interesting?" They call up a few directors to see if they have ideas, and then decide to postpone it for a season or two until the theatre's finances are in better shape.

Then, once we've committed to the play and lined up the rights and gone through a complex process of agreeing on a director, and then designers, we have roughly 4 months to go through step two, the design process, the goal of which is to complete a set of drawings in time for the technical team to assess the budget and plan the build.

At several points along the way, we do some casting, including one or two offers, some local auditions, and a trip to New York or Chicago. Finally, the full cast is called in for step three, rehearsals. These begin in the rehearsal hall for 3 or 4 weeks, and then continue on stage for another 1 week of tech, which is often the first time that all the artists are together in the same room. Then we have a few previews and scramble to make some final adjustments before our donors and critics arrive for opening night and a big shindig. We catch our breath for a day or two, and then turn our attention to the next play coming down the line.

It takes a theatre years to build up this capability. But hearing it described like this, it makes you wonder how we manage to get anything good on our stages at all. Somehow we do, and I think American theatre artists may be the best in the world at accomplishing so much in such a short time.

But if, as I suggested earlier, **innovation** happens with all the disciplines interacting together, driven by a shared purpose, then where on the assembly line do the actors, director, designers, and playwright come together to even talk about the purpose they might share together, and how they might approach this play any differently from the last one they worked on? Most especially, where on the assembly line can they have this conversation at a point where there are still innovative possibilities waiting to be discovered, and time to discover them?

So I've been wondering if we can somehow get a little bit more activity just off the assembly line, where the clock isn't ticking so loudly. And the paradigm shift that's starting to help me is this: What if, maybe not for every show, but for some of them, we shifted away from what I've called script search and development and toward a more holistic step I'd like the call **production development**, or maybe **purpose development**, right from the beginning of the process.

For example, if we're thinking we'd like to do a Chekhov play, can we gather a group of actors and designers together for a mini-workshop, read a couple of the plays, and ask them what it would mean to tackle Chekhov today? If we can't afford that, could we start this inquiry with some students or members of a think tank or local residents, maybe along with just three or four professional artists we'd like to work with? If it's a new play or adaptation, can we commission a group of collaborators working with the playwright on research, interviews, or other formative steps? To begin our design process, could we gather a few of our actors, whichever ones are already cast, and devise a workshop for them and the designers together?

Every time we create an opportunity, early in the process, for the entire team to work together, we dramatically increase the chances for both purpose and innovation. When we make the space for our artists to ask: what does this play mean to us, what does it mean to do it here and now, what are we trying to express to our audience—from there, it's a short step to asking: what could we do to surprise the heck out of our audience so they really sit up and listen. That's when innovation happens. That's when a production starts to have a point of view, a shared passion that goes beyond telling a story.

Sure, there are barriers: Schedules. Contracts. Dollars. The fact that so many of our freelance artists have to string one project to the next in order to make a living. Obviously, extra steps like these would be easier if every theatre had a resident company. But every production has a company, every city has an extended company of artists, and with even modest investments, we can transform their experience of working on plays, and energize our audiences.

While you've been listening, I hope you've been thinking what's quite obvious: steps like these are being taken at many American theatres, and in fact, some recent trends could make this an especially fruitful moment for theatrical innovation in our country. Generous funding flowing into the new play field, developmental partnerships and co-productions among many theatres, the mushrooming of new devising ensembles who work on a whole different model—all of these are creating opportunities for longer, deeper, more inclusive artistic processes. At Woolly Mammoth, for example, a special fundraising campaign called FREE THE BEAST has become a game-changer for how our artists engage together. You'll hear more examples from the colleagues joining me on stage in a few moments—practical strategies to gain control of the assembly line and make room for innovation.

At the new play convening I referred to earlier, Rocco Landesman famously said that there might be too many resident theatres. I don't agree, but I think there's an important caution. If our theatre buildings become homes for assembly lines that crank out too many plays, and if there isn't an opportunity for the artists working on those plays to develop a real sense of purpose, beyond just doing a good job and filling a slot in the season, then we're in trouble.

The most dangerous thing about the assembly line is not that it moves so fast, but that it just keeps moving, demanding more plays. We can deceive ourselves into thinking that if we just find the right plays, we'll find the right audiences; and in the short run that may be true. But in the long run, it's the purpose behind the plays we make, and the energy and invention with which that purpose is shared on the stage that galvanizes audiences. It's not just the stories we tell, but why and how we tell them that determines our success.

So, my conclusion is simple: theatrical innovation is the job of actors, directors, playwrights, designers, dramaturges, production managers, technical directors, and everyone else who works in our theatres. But creating the space for that innovation to happen—that is the job of artistic directors, managing directors, and other theatre leaders. And we may need some help from agents, unions, funders, and others, to shake up our model just a little bit, and give ourselves some flexibility in the way we gather artists together.

———

Our work in the American theatre today sits on top of two great revolutions. The first half of the 20th century saw a revolution of purpose whose goal was to more truthfully reflect the realities of American life. One of the great fruits of that revolution, *Death of a Salesman*, is on Broadway today. Its premiere in 1949 featured several veterans of The Group Theatre.

The second half of the 20th century saw a revolution of access, with the spreading of theatres across the landscape, and opening them to artists and audiences from many different backgrounds. All of us here today are a part of that revolution.

Perhaps we'll look back on the first half of the 21st century and see a revolution of process, with deeper collaborations among theatre artists leading to an explosion of innovation. Perhaps that revolution will get us closer to resolving the contradiction between "the advance of theatre as an art form and the discovery of new and larger audiences."

I'd like to offer five short theses about innovation. I hasten to add that I am not an expert or even a consultant on the topic of innovation, so I hope you will test and challenge these proposals vigorously. I also hope you'll forgive me for using a few examples from my own work, but they will help to illustrate my points.

1. First, a simple definition: **Innovation means working in new and different ways with the goal of achieving new and different results.** It is not the same as *creativity*, which I hope is a part of our work in the theatre every day. And it is not the same as *originality*, which I suppose is either part of our particular DNA as artists or not.

Innovation is more intentional than either of these. It comes from a conscious decision to try a new pathway you haven't tried before.

2. Second, **artistic innovation is relative to who you are, to what you've already done as an artist or a theatre, and to the specific community you work in.** In this regard, I find it useful to distinguish between Innovation with a big "I," and innovation with a little "i." For example, the introduction of Stanislavsky's ideas into the training of American actors had far-reaching consequences for the course of our theatre history, as did the decisions by Zelda Fichandler and Margo Jones to start professional companies outside of New York, as did the introduction of video to the stage. Big "I" innovations like these come along a few times each century. But just a few **weeks** ago, I tried a new approach to my first rehearsal for a new play—by dispensing with the usual table work and asking the actors to just get up on their feet and do the play. I'm hardly the first director to try this, but for me it was new, and it had far-reaching consequences for the way the show ultimately landed on our stage. Little "i" innovations like this are within reach every day. And I believe that the rare, big "I" innovations are only possible in a culture where little "i" innovations are happening quite often.

3. Third, **artistic innovation brings you closer to functioning like an artist, not just like a craftsperson or entertainer.** When you are thinking intentionally about how you would like to change or evolve the way you work, you are required to take a stance in relation to your own past work, in relation to the history of the field, and most of all, in relation to the world around you. Instead of asking "how can I do a good job on this play and make it work for my audience," you also start to ask, "what would it **mean** to do a good job on this play, why would it matter, what new ideas or approaches might help it matter?" Three years ago at Woolly, for example, we were starting to talk about civic discourse as the main *raison d'etre* of our work. Around the same time I was beginning to work on Bruce Norris' *Clybourne Park* and so I shared the new emphasis on civic discourse with our designers, and asked how the play could feel more like a civic conversation, not just a private one. This led to a simple but unexpected idea—to include a small section of audience members sitting on the stage, peering through the dining room window of the house where the play is set. This had a transformative effect on how our production was experienced by

the audience, and made the relevance of the play for our community quite palpable. Again, we were certainly not making theatre history by putting audience members on the stage. But for us, it was a novel and important artistic choice that grew from our specific purpose in doing the play. It gave us a sense of pride about our relationship as artists to the community around us. And three years later people are still talking about it.

4. Fourth, **artistic innovation deepens your relationship with your audience and supporters.** Instead of talking with them just about your upcoming shows or season, you can begin talking about the way your artistic process affects the character of your work, about your evolution and long-term goals as artists, your dreams for the kind of the theatre you hope to achieve in the future. This kind of dialogue enlists your supporters in the overall **project** that your theatre represents over time. It helps them understand the full range of your work including shows they don't especially like, and gives them a deeper connection to your more specific financial needs like higher artistic salaries and extra rehearsal time. At Woolly Mammoth, for example, we have started a special fund called "Free the Beast" which will invest in 25 plays over ten years and allow us to pay for long-term commissions, workshops, extra rehearsals, and company-building activities we couldn't previously afford. It took us a few years to effectively articulate the case for this fund, and it has not been the easiest money to raise. But it has absolutely deepened our connection with donors and audiences, allowed us to move closer to our ideal way of working, and made room for new artistic innovations.

5. Fifth, artistic innovation—because it comes from deep collaboration and significant trial and error—requires extra time and resources, and so **it is often dependent on other innovations in the areas of fundraising, marketing, financial management, etc.** The good news is that the effort to identify and articulate new innovations draws the artistic and the management sides of the theatre together in powerful ways, and makes everyone feel connected to the theatre's fundamental purpose. The bad news is that everyone has to get out of their silos, out of the crush of their everyday work, in order to figure out how to find the resources for innovation and overcome the obstacles that stand in the way.

I believe that the drive toward artistic innovation is worth the effort. It enhances our personal satisfaction as artists and keeps us fresh over time. It can galvanize and excite audiences and convince them of the vitality of our work. And it can help to position theatre more deeply within our culture, not just as a source of entertainment, but as an art form in dialogue with its own history and traditions, and with the society and the world around us.

Howard Shalwitz is Artistic Director of Woolly Mammoth Theatre Company, Washington, DC. This text was delivered as the Keynote Address at Theatre Communications Group (TCG) National Conference in Boston, Massachusetts—June 21, 2012, and includes additional text from 2nd keynote address delivered by Mr. Shalwitz at the 2013 TCG National Conference in Dallas, Texas for the Artistic Innovation and Artistry arc.

INNOVATION AND CATASTROPHE

John Biguenet

Innovation often precedes need. An experiment in style or structure that wins an audience may succeed, for the moment, through its novelty. But such innovation withers and is soon forgotten unless it takes root as a necessary convention in the depiction of ordinary experience—or at least of extraordinary experience.

Franz Kafka, for example, died unheralded in 1924, nearly two decades before many of his family were lost to the Holocaust. But that almost unthinkable horror as well as other twentieth-century bloodshed and state oppression seemed to demand a new kind of narrative, the type of story we have come to call "Kafkan." Though the anxiety Kafka rendered in his highly original novels and short fictions is immediately recognizable as an inescapable constituent of human consciousness, the author's stylistic innovations to capture his profound unease found a fertile bed in recent history.

His innovations grew into conventions that now extend beyond literature. When I was poet in residence at The University of Texas at Dallas, a local newspaper editorial decried a bureaucratic tangle citizens faced at City Hall as a "Chekhov-like" nightmare. The editorialist's error—he or she surely meant a "Kafka-like" nightmare— illuminates how complex is this process of metamorphosis from innovation to convention. Most educated readers would immediately grasp the implications of an allusion to Kafka in the critique of a bureaucracy. But even if acquainted with the plays of Chekhov, one would probably look up from the paper and a cup of morning coffee to ponder what exactly a "Chekhov-like" nightmare at City Hall would involve.

Though Chekhov's innovations have, I think, taken root as con- ventions of the modern stage, those methods of characterization and progressions of dialogue are far less obvious than the image of Kafka's monstrously transformed Gregor Samsa, scuttling around his bedroom to the consternation of both family and employers.

As was perhaps true with the work of Kafka, sometimes it takes a catastrophe for innovation to find its need.

When Vivian Mercier, writing in the *Irish Times* in 1956, insisted that Samuel Beckett had "written a play in which nothing happens, twice," she was speaking for her own time. The assumed nihilism of absurdist drama made sense to a generation shaped by both Modernist aesthetics and the Depression, the Second World War, and the Holocaust.

Half a century later, when a production of *Waiting for Godot* by the Classical Theatre of Harlem was presented among the ruins of New Orleans, audiences turned out literally by the thousands for the two performances. Few of those New Orleanians knew anything of the history of absurdism, nor did they imagine they had come to see a play about nothing. Instead, they sensed that Beckett's tale of two hapless individuals waiting for help that never arrives was a play written about the predicament in which they found themselves here in New Orleans two years after defective Federal levees had collapsed and destroyed the city.

The family of Wendell Pierce, one of the leads in the production, had lost everything in the flooding that followed Hurricane Katrina—as had most of those in the audience. Both actor and audience had paced the same ruined landscape as Vladimir and Estragon. In the Lower Ninth Ward and then in a second performance in Gentilly just a few blocks from my own mother's destroyed house, *Waiting for Godot* metamorphosed from a work of absurdism to a work of realism.

A year earlier, a draft of my first play to address the destruction of the city had been read at the 2006 National Showcase of New Plays, under the sponsorship of the National New Play Network. In *Rising Water*, a couple awaken in the middle of the night to find their pitch-dark house filling with water. Clambering into their attic, and then onto their rooftop, they struggle not only to survive but also to keep their love for each other alive. At the beginning of the second act, Camille has slipped through the hole her husband, Sugar, has cut onto the roof as the water continues to flood their attic. But Sugar is too large to fit any more than just his head through the jagged opening.

The audience of theater professionals at the showcase were quick to recognize my allusion to Beckett's *Happy Days*. In the talkback that followed the reading, they urged me to push the play even further in the direction of absurdism. But I had used the device of a bodiless head addressing a spouse not to create an absurdist play but to take advantage of the vocabulary that Beckett had established to depict two human beings isolated on a desolate plain without hope of help or the means to save themselves.

That vocabulary was a language immediately understood by New Orleanians in the early spring of 2007, when *Rising Water* opened at Southern Rep Theatre on the edge of the French Quarter. Located in a building that had been looted and burned in the chaotic days following the levee breaches, the theater still smelled of smoke the night the play opened just 18 months after the events it depicted. As would happen half a year later when Waiting for Godot was performed in the city, audiences waited in line to see the play. In fact, *Rising Water* became the bestselling show in the 20-year history of Southern Rep Theatre (despite the fact that the previous record was set when New Orleans had twice the population as the city did at the time of the play's run).

Rising Water and *Shotgun*, the second play in the trilogy *Rising Water* began, have now had 25 productions and staged readings around the country. Though the plays make use of absurdist tropes, no one has mentioned absurdism in writing about them. Just the opposite, audiences have commented on how the trilogy, like many other plays about historical events, are rooted in naturalism. But with the premiere of the final play in my trilogy, *Mold*, having closed just a few weeks ago, I can attest that Beckett was the playwright most useful to me in finding a way to depict terrible experiences for audiences who themselves had recently endured those events.

Writing three plays depicting the flooding of New Orleans and its aftermath has transformed my understanding of theater and how it differs from other forms of narrative. One of these insights about which I feel most confident is that once innovation finds its need, audiences no longer recognize it as new. Instead, they simply understand it as part of a language they have already been taught to speak. Unfortunately, it sometimes takes a catastrophe to discover such fluency.

John Biguenet is the author of seven books, including *The Torturer's Apprentice: Stories* and *Oyster,* a novel, as well as such award-winning plays as *The Vulgar Soul, Rising Water, Shotgun, Mold, Night Train,* and *Broomstick.* His Rising Water Trilogy will be published by LSU Press in 2015. *http://www.biguenet.com*

PULL FOCUS

Jeff McMahon

I am trying to pay attention to attention. Art is essentially that; an unimpeachable excuse to pay attention, to disregard distractions so as not to feel one is operating at a deficit. Art is not simply a notion, a gesture, but an action, slightly abstracted though requiring complete commitment. If you are in on the act (actually engaged in the work itself) or in it just for the money (whether collector, creator, or producer), you know why you are looking, listening, leaning in. But for the audience standing somewhat outside, staring through a window or devices pulling them not towards abstraction but distraction, there has to be some reward for that act of paying attention. Attention is hard work, and in some of our art, it is not clear what the payback is for that effort.

Artists pay attention to the fact that shared focus is shared currency. We struggle to find new exchanges, fresh ways to get rewarded for guiding others into this attentiveness. How much to pay, and to whom, and how? And how not to get distracted by the system of payment, an octopus tendering our attention even as the tentacles touch places we haven't paid enough attention to? We know what we want to do, but we are so distracted, even while finding new distractions to distract them (the audience, yet really ourselves) from those distractions. What's the attraction, the bait that makes delivery of our aestheticized attention worth the wait? Is what we offer really worth that much more than all the other distractions chewing on our scenery?

What attracts/distracts me now might well have bored you a while ago or will in the near future. What was clever on the page stumbles on the stage, and the brilliance of honeyed words runs like off-market ink when printed. What started as an arresting sound in the back of my throat dribbles out as the same old note held too long, a note not currently recognized as currency. So should we abandon the stage to a more fascinating projection, a screen that enlarges, edits who we are, and mashes us into media? Must I rig up a screen, project an image and amplified voice to slap you into attention? Once I have that, should I slyly lose the media? Is this mediating tendency merely a tactic for getting you to pay attention to the fundamentals of my story, my POV, my unique way of telling? Or is it because a blank sits where the story should be, and I am distracted by bells and whistles (there's the door!) even as I am trying to whistle louder? What might have been a new sound, a new look, too soon becomes the expected. And if it is expected, that expectant hope curdles into contempt; oh, that old thing again...

We trend towards devices small and portable, but with big effects. We tap the controls as an addict ups the dosage, and fiddle with our frequencies so as to never settle on a single clear channel. If only we didn't have to make such a spectacle! I know you would pay me the attention I deserve, if only I could plug you into my point-of-view. I fear you might be exhausted by the language required, so here's a series of choices you need not read too far into. We'll call it interactive, but the strategy is all mine.

Yes, we still must go to Moscow, we must find new forms (while making literate references to the old), must re-form and reload (non-violently) but jettison the jetpacks right after we break through the gravity barrier. We do this so we may speak normal to each other; a new normal, willing and able to focus on a line, a tone, a solitary figure, open-mouthed, telling us something we hadn't quite thought of. We just might hear it, see it plain as day in front of us, find our way in without all these... innovations.

We have gotten good at pointing pixels at our audience, electronically grabbing them by the eyeballs, pulsing our darting visions out to them in the form of athletically aesthetic entrainment. Movies move this way (though only in 2D), as it's in their form, while theatre took a while to pick up the gait. But now that we are all firing our neurons at the same time, can we change the picture? Should we use the same not-so-new tools to get our audience expanding their attention to the contemplative, the philosophic, work thick with layers and meaning? Can we still deliver our art chunky, weighted, wordy, and uncompressed?

Guest teaching in a colleague's class on Storytelling and Narrative, I felt myself oscillating between wanting to rip narrative asunder, yet wanting so much for a story to be told. I tend to expect tales to surprise me, not only narratively but aesthetically, formally. I snap to attention when the language of the work, the form of it, contains a subtle codex, a key, telling me how to figure it. That's the story, inseparable as our senses are from our bodies and brains. The Big Secret: it's very hard to tell a story, any story, without other strains contaminating and distracting and pulling focus. But now we are so hopped up, and hobbled, with hyperlinks that we can no longer follow the very linearity the avant-gardists pulled us out of.

Perhaps the innovation is to turn around and look, press rewind, not face directly forward. Visual artist James Nares says this about his own hour-long video installation, Street, shot in 2011 and exhibited at the Metropolitan Museum of Art in New York:

"My intention was to give the dreamlike impression of floating through a city full of people frozen in time, caught Pompeii-like, at a particular moment of thought, expression, or activity... a film to be viewed 100 years from now."

I experienced this work after seeing several portraits by the Italian quattrocento artist Piero della Francesca at the Frick Museum just down the street from the Met. Nares' contemporary work communicated with Piero through the basic technology of this one viewer's eyes and brain, committing to a mental/aesthetic re-curation, constantly mixing. Daily, we do and have this done to us digitally, but the original innovations in seeing (I am thinking of John Berger's analysis of looking and seeing) is that we humans bring so much into that sense. It's a busy street.

Both Piero and Nares stare at a subject, unlocking and yet re-arranging and staging what they are causing us to notice; Piero through paint and Nares through high-def, high-speed video. His camera, designed to capture actions so rapid that our eye cannot (a fired bullet, a hummingbird's wings), points outward from a vehicle traveling the streets of Manhattan. He moves laterally, tracking the sidewalk. When the film is projected, riding on and around the guitar-based score of Sonic Youth's Thurston Moore, Nares slows his subjects down, so slow that the banal gesture, the everyday movement of crowds in streets, slows the viewer down so that we may pay attention to our individuality and unity in the chaotic yet choral choreography of the city. Our shared gestures, which we did not know we shared, we share again because we are looking, watching. In the Nares work, the movement, and the overall direction, follows a pointing hand, a running child, a floating bubble, as the car holding the camera moves inexorably forward on a track that cannot make adjustments. As in Piero's painting, we more fully see what and who is there, through this retarding and reworking of the "real." The present communicates with the past, acknowledges the hand-over, the flow of ideas and sensation. This visual installation innovates for our eyes and not for "unique" commodity value, causing us to look back at ourselves while time pushes us forward.

Focus, being a prime component of the very apparatus of media, is taken as a given in film, but how to achieve this in an exhibit, or a piece of live theatre? The innovation of media has matured, allowing us to move both backwards and forwards, cradling our attention. In most theatre such a mediating element remains somewhat external. For now. Yet innovation does not only lunge forward but hops side-to-side and backwards, engaging us in a multidirectional dance in which we may not always feel in control. It can be dizzying, as it's not clear what we should be focusing on; where is the ground, where is the sky, which walls are illusory and which are real? Can we who work in theatre achieve equilibrium as we focus both on the action on our own street, and look to the vanishing point down the road? It can be radical to go back to the roots, but it also gets us dirty again. Have we fully integrated, critically, the word with the gesture, the action with the reflection, and the apparatus with the action? Are we sharing our street with media, or have we let it be repaved as a projection, blurring our liveness? The surface needs to be kept hot, malleable, constantly reshaped, as we reclaim the right-now over the recorded. If our own innovations leave us standing, stunned, overwhelmed by our wonder at them more than through them, we will be left muted and unmoved. Attention must be paid.

Jeff McMahon is a writer and performer and Associate Professor in the School of Film, Dance & Theatre, Arizona State Univ. Lives in Arizona and New York. MFA from the Writing Program, School of the Arts, Columbia University, and BA in Interdisciplinary Art from SUNY/Empire State College.
http://www.jeffmcmahonprojects.net/wordpressblogjeff/

ON THE VIRTUES OF 'OPEN SOURCE' INNOVATION IN THE ARTS

Duška Radosavljević

I am going to argue that artistic innovation is an overrated concept. More specifically, my view is that, contrary to business innovation perhaps, innovation in the context of the arts cannot be a valid goal. I want to underline this because I find it surprising how often the expectation seems to be that for something to have true artistic value it has to be seen to be innovative. And conversely, disappointment often ensues when something that was expected to be innovative proves not to be so.

One criticism leveled at the Belgian theatre collective Ontroerend Goed[1], for example, has been that aspects of their work had already been seen or done before. For those who don't know it, a significant part of Ontroerend Goed's oeuvre (*The Personal Trilogy, Audience*) has attracted attention because of its inventive engagement of the audience as part of the inner structure—and sometimes even the very core—of the work itself.[2]

The point I like to make in response to such accusations is that if you look closely, in fact, (successful) artists rarely set out to be innovative. Innovation is an inevitable byproduct of their other concerns. Picasso's paintings were not a result of a desire to shock or offer something new for its own sake, but a result of a thoughtful engagement with the world around himself. Working on the cusp of a paradigm shift between representational and conceptual art, Picasso was able to go in step with his time and express this in his work. Similarly with Ontroerend Goed, the creative impulses behind each piece the company has made are a direct result of their quest to engage with the world around them

---

[1] Ontroerend Goed's website: *http://www.ontroerendgoed.be/projects.php.*

[2] Cathy Turner and I have called this kind of work which depends on the input of the audience 'porous dramaturgy' (*http://humanities.exeter.ac.uk/drama/ research/projects/porousdramaturgy/*), although we apply the definition to a much broader range of practices.

and offer their own artistic response to it.[3] Often the questions they wish to tackle are simple (e.g. "How quickly can you form a meaningful relationship with a stranger" for Internal) and their artistic approach is primarily metatheatrical in nature—that is, concerned with exploring the form itself. This might perhaps be explained by the fact that most of the company members were literature graduates who fell into theatre-making through performance poetry and their examination of the form, arising out of a personal necessity, remained largely unencumbered by theoretical concerns. But, yes—even despite the fact that their work has given me a completely new and fresh kind of theatre experience on more than one occasion[4]—I would agree that there is nothing new about the way they make theatre. Some aspects of their and other interactive theatre companies' work can be traced right back to the mystery plays, and maybe even to ancient Greece. This only seems new to us, arguably, because we have been blinkered by a century of sitting quietly in theatres behind the "fourth wall."

It seems that we are on the cusp of another paradigm shift as far as theatre is concerned, or at least I hope so. And in this perhaps we are lagging behind science already. In the early 2000s, the Finnish physicist and former Nokia research scientist, Ilkka Tuomi developed an interesting thesis for his book *Networks of Innovation* (2001, 2006), based on the idea that innovation, like knowledge itself, is a social product, contingent on the involvement of a "community." This principle was made particularly obvious by the advent of the internet and the philosophical shift towards the "Open Source" development model in technology, where networks of software writers were being enabled to add to the development of a particular product thus replacing the previously used linear model of closely guarded corporate secrets. This change of outlook came about as a result of the realization that many technological innovations (such as the telephone, the internet and email) had acquired their significance and popularity because of the user initiative, rather than because of the original goal with which they were created. Thus one of Tuomi's conclusions is that

---

[3] I devote a large part of the final chapter of *Theatre-Making* (2013) to analyzing the genesis of The Personal Trilogy.

[4] I initially wrote about my experience of Internal in 2009 here: *http://postcardsgods.blogspot.co.uk/2009/09/guest-post-duskaradosavljevic-on.html*.

"innovation happens in periphery" even though "such peripheries are conventionally described as frontiers" (2001).

It is interesting that this theoretical interest in the notion of "community" in the field of epistemology and science—which Tuomi traces back to Jean Lave and Etienne Wenger's 1991 title *Situated Learning: Legitimate Peripheral Participation*—notion of "community" was largely discredited in the Humanities due to its association with the dogmas of the then failed ideology of communism. We in the arts have therefore shied away from the concept of community while the scientists were able to redefine and understand it as something that does not emerge from putting together a sufficient number of individuals. On the contrary, individuals became persons with individual identities through their membership in the various communities they are members of. (Tuomi, 2001)

This is related to the French philosopher Jean-Luc Nancy's idea of "community" as a collection of individuals "being together" which he posed as far as 1986, but it has taken a while for this to really reach those of us in the arts. Our temporary estrangement from the positive aspects of "being together" perhaps explains why we have remained stuck with the idea that the individual artist has to be the one who innovates (rather than this being a process which involves the user, or a process which involves community). It also explains why the biggest enemy of artistic innovation is the artist's own ego—but that's another story altogether.

Duška Radosavljević is a dramaturge, writer and scholar based at the University of Kent, UK. She is the editor of *The Contemporary Ensemble: Interviews with Theatre-Makers* (Routledge, 2013) and the author of *Theatre-Making: Interplay Between Text and Performance in the 21st Century* (Palgrave, 2013).

ARTS ENTREPRENEURSHIP: YOU ARE CLOSER THAN YOU THINK.

Jim Hart and Gary D. Beckman

"My second conclusion is that attributes of creative individuals and attributes of entrepreneurs are so similar that even attempting to define a set of predetermined characteristics is a futile exercise."
(Bygrave & Zacharakis The Portable MBA for Entrepreneurship)

No doubt by now, we have all heard about the Arts in relation to Entrepreneurship. So, what is it, how do we do it and who benefits?

In its most basic configuration, arts entrepreneurship concerns earning a 21st century living from one's art. Philosophically, the term speaks to how art can impact audiences and communities. For artists, it is about manifesting the empowerment creative autonomy promises. The premise is simple: artists possess the temperament and skills to not only act entrepreneurially, but they can enjoy the same benefits as any entrepreneur.

The purpose of this article is to briefly explore how—as creative professionals—we possess both the skills to make an entrepreneurial living with our art and that we may have a responsibility to ourselves and those who follow to take responsibility for changing how we manifest our Art as professionals. Some might deem this a "call to action" and that is exactly what this article suggests.

Shared, Embedded and Honed Skills

Theatre—as a discipline, Art form, industry and community can lead the way in this emerging discipline of Arts Entrepreneurship as it exists both in higher education and professionally. The training we undertake is (perhaps without most participants' knowledge) preparing us for a possible life as an entrepreneur.

Most in the business of theatre begin in an acting class. Acting is the window into the industry and from there, many either leave the industry, continue acting or find new talents, passions and interests like directing, writing, producing or designing.

In theatre training, we do not learn just acting, but explore front of the house to the back of the house. We do practicum: hanging lights, working in a costume shop, selling tickets, answering phones on occasion, and building and striking sets. We do it all: we don't just play one role, we make Theatre. "Entrepreneurs" do the same thing; they just make "Business Theatre"—the overarching premise in Pine and Gilmore's 2011 tome, "The Experience Economy."

For example, the improvisation classes we take develop a sensitivity to imagination and impulses. We learn how to say, "Yes" and to follow impulses without fear, judgment or resources. We find ourselves acting with others in highly bizarre and complex scenarios that we have to "act" our way through. Entrepreneurs, similarly, often find themselves in such situations and must rely on quick thinking, problem solving and the following of impulses.

Further, the storytelling skills we learn as performers, play well into branding ourselves as an artist, entrepreneur or arts business. The research skills we use to research a play or character can simply be repurposed to research one's market and competition. Our understanding and experience in collaboration aids us in building a culture around creative businesses that represents values: personal, professional, political, artistic, etc. Just like we cast plays, entrepreneurs hire employees.

The self-discipline we develop from long nights and countless hours of rehearsal help us execute the determination and endurance to plan and build creative businesses—even if the business is an actor alone, a business of one. The hardships we endure with lines, difficult emotions on stage, previews before a live audience, being vulnerable and open, etc.—these seemingly theatre-specific skills are also entrepreneurial skills. Entrepreneurs use these skills in working with others as they grow and direct the business they create.

As a collaborative art form, Theatre cannot be created alone. One must have at least one actor and at least one audience member. Similarly, an entrepreneur must have customers. (This being better conceived as an audience member). But as we know, theatre requires more than just two. It involves many individuals who are often working in the background, seemingly unnoticed, but nonetheless vital to the process. No entrepreneur builds a business alone. Entrepreneurs need others to manifest "Business Theatre" just like theatre artists.

Those in the Theatre Arts are skilled in collaboration, taking direction (adaptability) and vision building (creating something out of nothing). We have skills in problem solving in the moment, in selling ourselves, which we learn through auditions. In brief, theatre artists are the ideal candidates to show other artists how a living can be made in the arts as so many of our basic skills are specifically entrepreneurial skills. For most theatre artists, they are in the theatre business as any typical entrepreneur is in "Business Theatre."

Many artists feel that they are, at their essence, artists; entrepreneurs feel similarly; the act of "entrepreneuring" is an art. Meaning and passion fuel creativity and drive through the difficult and lean times. Entrepreneurs are also creators. But rather than focusing on the creation of a character, they manifest a vision and value as they recognize and realize opportunity. They create jobs and in the process, stimulate the economy.

What becomes necessary for these creatives, once they discover the parallels between their innate theatrical skills and the skills of entrepreneurship (or "Business Theatre"), is to acquire those skills absent from their college training (budgeting, business plan creation, fundraising, etc.). All of this can be taught and are practiced by artists every day.

Action, Action, Action

Imagine a new standard in arts education that incorporates the entrepreneurial ethos into artistic training. In such training, we empower our artists, our sensitive souls, dreamers, visionaries, myth-makers and storytellers with entrepreneurial skills. What are entrepreneurial skills? It involves manifesting the empowerment creative autonomy promises. Such skills serve an individual in life, just as they do in art and entrepreneurship.

There is a Movement Underway. What is this Movement? It is one of mass autonomy for emerging artists, working artists and creative visionaries. Autonomy is self-governance, independence, and self-sufficiency. Entrepreneurial skills are also that of creativity, imagining, envisioning, all skills that are just like that of the artist.

We ask you to act for, with and through this effort. In the interest of brevity and directness, below is a pseudo-FAQ:

What Makes this a Movement? Today there are approximately 96 colleges and universities offering programs in Arts Entrepreneurship and they appear to be springing up at once. Note that private support is helping to fund the movement; Jimmy Iovine and Dr. Dre gave the University of Southern California a $70 Million dollar gift, part of which is to train artists in entrepreneurship. Harvard has an initiative, Juilliard does too, as well as MIT and Southern Methodist University's Meadows School of the Arts and others, like the University of Texas at Austin, North Carolina State University and the University of Arizona's P.A.V.E. program. In fact, it's international:

South Africa: Re-dreaming the economy: why creative entrepreneurs are the future

Great Britain: Kickstarter entrepreneurs doing big business in the UK

Australia: Not a dirty word: Arts entrepreneurship and higher education

Why should I join? Learn some new tools that might be missing in your creative arsenal. Learn about a new, developing artistic discipline. Participate in the dialog and your voice becomes part of what defines this Movement and Arts Entrepreneurship in the classroom, on stage and in communities.

Who should participate? Working artists, entrepreneurs, academics, new and emerging arts students, observers and those who seek to learn about the Movement all can play a role.

How do I become a part of the Movement? If you could create anything, regardless of resources, what would you create? Who would benefit? Where do they live and how could you get a message to them? How would your experience and embedded entrepreneurial skills impact your community, emerging artists, the Movement and Art itself?

There are many ways you can participate, starting small. Piloting an arts venture is typically easy, low risk and low cost. Something simple like the "pop up shop" model is always helpful. Perhaps there is a small work you've always wanted to direct but were stymied by the costs? Renting unused commercial space to act as a temporary theatre for two weeks is ideal in this case. Securing in-kind donations for staging materials, costumes and perhaps the space itself is a great way to get to know your local business community and secure future partners. (Donations may be tax deductible, so businesses are actually incentivized to help). Are you for-profit? Seek fiscal sponsorship through organizations like Fractured Atlas. Then, partner with a local college or university's theatre department as there are plenty of in-training, enthusiastic and creative collaborators eager to build their resume. Make sure to document your process and creative works with high quality digital recordings (both sound and audio). The materials you document (video, audio, image, text, etc.) can serve as material for content creation. The key to entrepreneurship is to start. If you enjoy the process, your first attempt will likely not be your last and just as your talents in Theatre have grown over time, so too will your entrepreneurial skills.

Information is out there, but the best information available is from currently working everyday entrepreneurs. They will have great stories, wisdom and value to share.

Or, if you possess some significant arts experience, you can mentor an emerging artist—either through Art, how to succeed in the profession or how to raise funds. Call a local university and offer a master class or a weekend workshop that shares your existing entrepreneurial and professional skills to those aspiring to the profession. If there are higher education Arts Entrepreneurship efforts locally (see this link for the most up-to-date list) call the director and offer to guest lecture. Take Arts Entrepreneurship courses at these institutions; instructors typically find a much richer experience for students and working artists learn cutting edge ways to reach younger audiences. Explore this toolbox for arts entrepreneurs. Truly, to act within the Movement is limited only by one's own creativity.

Once the necessary step of beginning has been taken, do what is most necessary right now. Then, do the most pressing and necessary thing next. Make a plan. Set goals daily and if you don't accomplish them, don't despair—but move them to the next day's goals. The self-discipline we develop in theatre makes a successful artist in this game of entrepreneurship.

Next, find an audience. Create for them. Initiate a dialog and help them feel a part of your creative process, as they will engage in the process again. Learn about the community. Work with people. Ask what they need and serve their needs. Build so much goodwill around the actions of "entrepreneuring" Art that communities want to contribute.

Think about your audience and create for them. Think about your available skills, talents, experiences and interests (especially interests) and imagine them repurposed. Get into a war generation mind frame— be frugal and thoughtful about available resources and needs. Just as Stanislavsky taught us to pursue our needs, serving others' needs leads to being necessary and being necessary can lead to profitability, value, more Art and most importantly, autonomous artists.

Wasn't this started in the 70's? The seeds were indeed and we owe much to those who have paved the path for this emerging field. We stand upon their shoulders. Arts Entrepreneurship is nothing new, as artists have known for ages, but the structuring of an academic field is new.

Come join us. Join the Movement.

Jim Hart serves as Director of Arts Entrepreneurship at Meadows School of the Arts, Southern Methodist University. Hart founded The International Theatre Academy Norway (TITAN Theatre Academy), a two-year accredited conservatory for Theatre Entrepreneurship in Oslo, Norway. Hart directs, acts, produces and writes in addition to a wide range of entrepreneurial pursuits. Hart earned his M.F.A.

in Acting from the Yale School of Drama and holds a BFA in Theatre/ Acting from SMU.

Gary D. Beckman is Director of Entrepreneurial Studies in the Arts at North Carolina State University where he developed and administers the nation's first campus-wide Arts Entrepreneurship Minor. He earned a Ph.D. in Musicology from The University of Texas at Austin, a M.A. in Musicology from the University of New Hampshire and a B.A. in Music from the University of Southern Maine. At UT Austin, he was principle investigator the first nation-wide study of arts entrepreneurship efforts in higher education, funded by the Ewing Marion Kauffman Foundation. This work remains the only national study of Arts Entrepreneurship programs.

AGENTS OF CHANGE

Dominic D'Andrea

A professor in graduate school asked me a question, which challenged the entire way I view my purpose in the theatre. The question was: "What is your business?" Without knowing what she was getting at, I replied, "Well, I'm a director, and I run a theatre festival." She said to me, "No, you see, you just told me your profession. That is your job. What is it that you aim to do through your work besides make money and survive? Let me reframe the question: *What are you in the business of?* Just because your job is in the theatre, doesn't automatically mean you get to be an agent of change. Your answer just tells me you have a gig. If you are going to do anything of lasting value for other people with this work, you have to know what your business is." It took me a long time to unpack her offering. I'm still thinking through what this all means.

The term *agent of change* has been thrown around a lot lately on twitter, blog posts, and especially in an over-shared Facebook meme via a quote from a famous Hollywood actor (which was the inspiration for this post, btw.) It's arguable that the ideology behind this term is rooted in Paulo Freire's principles of a humanizing pedagogy, and was applied to theatrical vocabulary in Augusto Boal's work. The concept of existing as an agent of change holds sacred meaning for many theatre artists connected to theatre for social justice, community-engaged theatre, educational theatre, and other "applied theatre" modes of work that are often given less attention than the new play sector, and systems of development and production of plays we as a field talk about so much. Only recently has the term started to be used in our wider artistic lexicon, as evident by the Facebook memes, twitter chatter, etc.

For me, serving as an agent of change means subscribing to a belief in a radical humanizing pedagogy, identifying and naming systems of oppressors and the oppressed, a commitment to being person or participant-centered in artistic modes of engagement, and offering the tools necessary for individuals and groups to make necessary changes through love, dialogue, education, understanding, repetition, commitment, and identifying critical changes of appraisal. It is a skill set, a learned behavior, and a lived attitude. Being an agent of change is a business many artists are in, but it is a way of life that has to be learned, practiced, shared, reflected upon, refined, reapplied, and paid forward in order to be earned. We may work as actors, directors, writers, dramaturges, or artistic leaders, but our agency helps define who we are and what we stand for. Personally speaking, I do not take this point lightly. I believe one has to self-identify as having earned this sense of agency through prolonged practice, a body of work, and concrete results; however, it is a welcome and obtainable goal that one can—and probably should—aspire to if working in the theatre. Subscribing to these beliefs won't require membership to an exclusive club, but probably will require a great deal of commitment, and a long period of growth and adjustment. It's an attitude and one has to want it.

As practitioners, artists, and stakeholders in the American theatre, we have an immense hunger to make the world a better place through attempts at innovation, re-evaluating our methods of working, and engaging in new modes of collaboration and audience engagement. Our best intentions are articulated in our company meetings, in our collaborations, and in our ongoing social media conversations. I don't think any of us have ever heard of artists being in the theatre to promote sentiments of chaos, hate, and destruction. (If they do exist, I'd love to hear about what that looks like.)

On the other hand, it's no secret that many of us have experienced a lasting frustration towards institutions and gatekeepers who are not doing enough to combat the underrepresentation of artists of color, women, underrepresented points of view, early career artists, alternative artists. Almost every statistic published about what is being represented on our stages points to a culture riddled with great imbalances. I have yet to see one bit of research that concludes we are even in the cultural ballpark of getting it right; however, for every condemning statistic there are just as many brilliant cultural combatants and innovators, who are constantly introducing new ideas that promote change. There is a lot of good work happening, an abundance of good ideas bubbling up, and an army of capable artists, leaders, and trendsetters, doing awe-inspiring pitch-perfect work responding to the greater need.

The other side of this coin: decision makers, gate keepers, and institutional stakeholders who choose to ignore these overwhelming calls to action for great change become active participants in one of the most dangerous systems of oppression: apathy. Those in power who subscribe to casual mantras like "that's just the way it is", or "I don't see a reason to change" have some serious soul searching to do. It is important to name these instances when they happen, if we are to create realistic conditions for change and innovation. Many of our artists experience the impact of these power dynamics on an ongoing basis. Most of us don't get paid well, if at all, we stay in the field against all odds because of ideas and the people, and the hope that maybe— just maybe—something that we do or make will make a difference to somebody. We all hope for the opportunity to have our voices be heard in meaningful ways, despite a lack of resources, time, and (frankly) of interest by large portions of our culture at-large.

These days, questions of agency have become core to many ongoing conversations about changing the American theatre. Finding ways to contextualize these ideas, and implementing reasonable ways put them into action has become our task. The demand for change is a radical act in and of itself. Change starts by naming oppressive elements, and works to find new and important pathways to results that are beneficial for many. The results of these efforts are the product, and perhaps those results are concrete examples of innovation left as our cultural artifacts. *Change* is our business. *Innovations* are what we accumulate along the way.

So, applying this to the original question: *What am I in the business of?* I took this prompt upon myself as a call to action. It propelled me to re-define my actions, helped me to be more self-critical about the choices that I make, and to look at the conditions in which I engage with people and projects.

Yes, I am a director, and I do run an ongoing national theatre festival called *The One-Minute Play Festival*, and for a few years, I also struggled to put myself through graduate school, while not going broke. We've all been there at one time or another: working and putting ourselves through school, and that's just the way that it goes. It's an old story, and common to the experience of many of us. These are conditions related to my *job* in the theatre.

My *business*, however, is a different kettle of fish altogether. My business is informed and measured by my values, my actions, and the impact these actions have on those around me. My business is a set of ideas that I am responsible for upholding for myself, and offering to the wider world to engage in. I am in the business of community engagement, dialogue, and consensus building *through* the work that I do. I don't just produce a theatre festival, but take the opportunity to make it a convening that becomes an artistic and social barometer project.

The work I do with the One-Minute Play Festival serves as a perfect example of how simple adjustments in thought and action can provoke meaningful changes. When I started producing #1MPF, what is fast approaching a decade ago, it was a modest experimental short-form theatre festival, which we did as an annual event in New York City. The main value it held was that it was a lot of fun. Above and beyond the very large community it brought together, and the fun of seeing a bunch of really quick works, it was not very meaningful, nor did it have a clear set of goals and objectives.

I recognized that there was value to the work: participants would be overjoyed to participate each year, and we collectively learned so much from seeing all of the playwrights' offerings. It took me four years of mechanically producing this event every year, to begin to get the right idea.

After an opportunity presented itself to travel to a regional theatre on a LORT contact and to then "tour" the work, I had a simple revelation that re-defined the entire reason for which the festival existed: *it's about the community in which it serves*. It occurred to me that in a tour model no one would really care about the work out of context, and it didn't really have the same meaning to us engaged in the work. The buy-in is, was, and continues to be that #1MPF is a community event that examines local topics and idea. It was as simple as that. If the model changed from community event, to touring model, the core-value of the work is completely diminished. It would mean involving artists, designers, and others who were not involved in the creation of the work, or its community culture.

Of course, I ended up declining to go on tour, and decided that if I was going to do this work in different cities, I would have to do it exactly the same way I did it in NYC: with, for, by, and about local artists and investigating local topics and ideas. Once I made the commitment to begin working in ways focused on local activity, and put those ideas out into the world, things happened immediately—and in the right ways. The tradeoff is that working in an idea-driven, and not a profit-driven model, meant that it would be a project with no budget, and little or no financial return. I recognized this path was not going to be as successful financially, but offered an opportunity to build on the ideas and integrity we established and wanted to see nurtured.

I began to work in a series of national partnerships with orgs and leaders I had relationships with who were paying attention to the work, and invited me to come and play. The festival formalized from event into a full-out *company*, and a new hybrid partnership model emerged that we are still using today: it's part community convening, part play festival, part platform for an exchange of ideas.

Today, #1MPF serves as a barometer project examining and highlighting important ideas that emerge across the collective consciousness of artists in specific communities. We use the image of a core sample or a performed community mind-map to describe what the work is all about, or an accumulation of pulses of stories. #1MPF partners exclusively with playwright or community engaged theatres, which support service-based programming to various degrees. We engage playwrights living and working in local communities through consensus reached between the institution, and local artists outside of the institution. While we occupy the halls of many influential institutions, we attempt to avoid an institutional narrative of which voices are most important, and to get at who and what is really there. We get this right to varying degrees, and learn from our mistakes and accumulated knowledge. We invite the writers into a playmaking process that prompts them to offer brief moments that are without a prescribed theme. I ask them to write based on what they are thinking about and responding to at the present moment in time, and we examine what themes/ideas/values emerge across the spectrum of the work, and we look at how best to highlight these ideas. In addition to the production side of the work, we (as a community) engage in dialogue and consensus building community sessions with artists and the wider community that explore central questions like *who are we? What is our relationship to each other? To our community? To our work?*

We identify assets, deficits, bright spots, topics, and issues relevant to this particular group of people at this moment in time. We occupy the halls of these institutions for a moment of time, make art, hang out, and are with one another. We challenge the institutional leadership to listen to what is being offered by the artists, and see if they can identify ways to be of service to their community once the festival's time is over. We hold each artist and member of institutional leadership to be accountable for what they offer, by naming actions they could take to uphold their "contract" with the community. (These needs look different in each case.)

Most of the money we raise through for our partnering institutions is earmarked to give back to playwright, educational, or community specific programming in all cases. They may not simply use the money for operating costs, unless that is an agreed upon need. They must use it to give back to a need in their community. We supported youth summer programs, playwright residency programs, teaching artists working in economically challenged communities and prisons, second stage/off night artist space grants, free ticket programming, a fledgling playwrights' communication group, commissions, internship programs, and other types of programming that are service oriented.

We've been able to do a lot of good in small doses for local causes. The kicker: we've done almost all of this without *any kind* of real budget. We've raised thousands upon thousands of dollars for programs that support and/or promote change, growth, development, or education. A lot of times, artists are gifting their time entirely, so we condense the time period and number of performances, as to respect their time, and not take advantage of their gifts—it takes the form of a special event, and an opportunity to occupy a space. We are not greedy or driven by financial return, and we try to respect those boundaries with our artists. We keep the mission or program we are supporting with each festival as a centerpiece, so every artist knows why they are there, and what they are working towards. This work is community forward, which means, money or not, the focus is on engagement. We are happy just to get people in the room together speaking. As long as people want to engage in this work, it remains relevant. In the last several years #1MPF has grown from an annual event in NYC, to thirteen annual events in different cities. By leading with ideas of community engagement and dialogue, we've tapped into something that feels necessary and of this moment. When it stops being that, I will stop doing the work, and examine all exit strategies available to me to best honor the work that we've done.

To be transparent: At #1MPF, I am one person, who works with one staffer, a producing fellow, and a couple of interns; and, I have two or three artists who serve occasionally as curators or festival directors. I have a series of partnering national producers. We also partner with Howlround.com and HowlroundTV, which streams and archives our work. We are a movement, not an institution. We have no budget. We are not supported by grants. We depend on our partners for support. The work we do always makes money, despite the odds, and the money is used for concrete change. In that way, it's a brilliant model, and the innovation comes in the ways in which we engage with the communities and the institutions. We have never been to a city that we have not been invited back to to play again. This year, we are adding a bunch of new cities, as we've grown to 24 national partnerships. We are now producing year round without a break.

I deeply value the relationship I have with each institution and each community of artists as a time investment that will be made over a period of several years. The result is that I feel a part of many different local communities, and I also feel I serve as a seasonal staff member at nearly two-dozen different theatres. Collectively, we've been able to learn and experience a lot about local culture from being inside of it.

We offered artists an opportunity to express themselves in ways they might not normally get to in their regular flow of life. I feel I have accumulated what is probably an accurate picture of what the American theatre looks like from local perspectives. Above all I feel the work we've made continues to work towards creating the space for dialogue; exchange of ideas; affirming assets, deficits, and beliefs; and, creating the conditions for artists to take actions to make changes themselves and for their communities. The degrees of these changes vary, and because they happen on a hyper-local level, I tend to hear about them when artists email me and let me know that the idea they discussed is now in action, or that the project with the collaborator they met in the festival is happening, or the institution decided to let artists use the space for free, or new community partnerships have formed with service orgs in the various cities—senior centers, youth populations, and cultural/religious groups.

I opted to expand on what we have done with #1MPF to point out a simple concept: as an artist and as a human being struggling with my purpose, I had to define my agency. I could be in the business of just producing a theatre festival (and that's fine), or I could be in the business of creating community engagement, dialogue, and consensus building through the medium of producing a theatre festival: the latter has worked in service of an idea: to create the conditions for change. I didn't want a *gig*. I wanted *purpose*. #1MPF is one example among many movements that has a conscious sense of agency.

In closing, I'd like to take this opportunity to challenge you (the reader) to think about and identify some of the companies, individuals, and current movements in the field who are achieving meaningful innovations through a commitment to radical change. Who do you feel makes a difference? Who are your heroes? What are they doing that you consider meaningful, innovative, or necessary? And for yourselves: What can you do? What voids do you see in your community? How can you fill-in those voids? What does being of service look like? What assets do you see? What challenges do you experience? And how can you turn challenges into action, action into a path, a path into a movement, and a movement into a series of results? How can you accumulate innovations along the way? What do you want to do? What business are you in? Please! Go out into the world. Live in a way that leads with your values. Do something different. It's the only way we'll create the conditions for meaningful and lasting change.

Dominic D'Andrea is the founder and producing artistic director of the One-Minute Play Festival (#1MPF.) He has led over 60 national festivals in partnerships with Primary Stages, Victory Gardens, Cornerstone Theatre Company, Playwrights Foundation, INTAR Theatre, Mixed Blood, InterAct Theatre, Round House Theatre, Oregon Shakespeare Festival and many others. He was a 2012 *NewYorkTheatre.com* person of the year, is a member of the Lincoln Center, Chicago, and Los Angeles Directors Labs, and is a faculty member of ESPA at Primary Stages. He is a graduate work at CUNY's Applied Theatre Program and The University of Maryland, College Park.

ACT TWO
BEING WITH

WHAT CAN WE DO?

Andy Smith

A performer walks into a theatre, sits down on a chair on an otherwise empty stage, and after a moment's silence reveals to the gathered audience that their intention is to present a work about how they can change the world. After relaying thoughts about all of the methods they considered using in order to achieve this—the lights and technology they might have employed, the many scenes they could have written, the different characters that could have appeared, the other titles that they have considered—the performer discloses that perhaps one of the best things the assembled might do in the present circumstances is actually just sit together quietly for a bit, maybe listen to the sound of their breathing.

Let's say that in another work, the same performer steps out of the audience and walks onto the stage. They take a position in front of a music stand that holds a scrapbook, open it, and proceed to read the text it contains. For the next forty-five minutes or so they read a simple story about a group of people who have gathered together in a room somewhere—a room that looks a bit like the one the performer and audience are in—to listen to a story. The story tells stories about what it might be that has brought these people there, about what the potential of the situation is, about what they might all do when the story ends.

These short synopses describe *all that is solid melts into air* and *commonwealth*, two works for theatre spaces that form the practical component of a research project that I have been undertaking for the last three years. They represent the ongoing development of a practice that I have been involved in making since 2003 and that I call a *dematerialized* theatre. This is a theatre that—inspired by the conceptual art practices of the late sixties and early seventies from which it takes its name—looks to try and do more with less. It's a theatre resistant to the construction of places and things. I'm not interested in making a spectacle, rather in building something simple and everyday with modest means. This is a theatre that may appear small, but it wants to think big.

A *dematerialized theatre* takes ideas from examples like Michael Craig Martin's seminal artwork *An Oak Tree, 1973*. You may know this work. It consists of a glass of water on a shelf, underneath which a text is installed on the wall that contains a dialogue between the artist and an imaginary viewer. The text explores the processes that allowed the artist to do what he claims to have done, which is alter the accidents of the glass of water so that it is no longer a glass of water, but an oak tree.

In 2005 this work inspired and lent its name to a play I co-directed by my friend, the writer and actor Tim Crouch. This play tells a story of two characters, but one of the actors playing one of those characters is new every night. They step out from the audience at the start having never seen or read the work, and having been encouraged by us to find out as little as possible about it as they can. At the beginning, without costume or accent or any of the rehearsal or preparation that we might have expected a performer to have undertaken, through a series of simple suggestions not unlike those that Craig-Martin uses to alter the accidents of the glass of water in his artwork, this actor is transformed into the character that they play, an act of transformation that, simply through the application of some chosen words, takes place in the audience as much as in the actor. It's an act made possible in the context and conditions created by us and the black box theatre in the same way I understand the white walls of the gallery allow Craig-Martin and his viewer to change a glass of water into an oak tree.

In my later practice and research, I have in part been trying to see if I can reduce an act of theatre even further. Remove all excess until I am left with something very basic, and in many ways very traditional, but something that I still hope holds the potential to be essential. Here I am sitting and talking to an audience. Here I am standing and talking to an audience. Here we are. Still undertaking something like—as Craig-Martin has reflected in relation to the glass of water on the shelf—an act of faith: the faith of an artist in their capacity to speak, and the belief of an audience in accepting what they have to say.

But here's the thing. I think that by being in the room with an audience, by being together with some other people in the social environment of the theatre, I am not alone in this capacity. By undertaking these particular acts, and using what we have got, I want to try and create opportunities for us all to think about what any of us might have to say. I want to do this so that we might all ask what we do, and can do in relation to making the theatre that we are all involved in making. We are all involved. I want to ask if we might still think and see theatre spaces as spaces of capacity, spaces where it doesn't take us much to think about how we are acting and how we might act. How we are able to regard and in some way alter the accidents of things. How we might take inspiration and courage from the acts of transformation that I think the theatre can offer us and that we participate in, and make the space to consider how we can apply some of its ideas to the worlds beyond its doors.

Key to both my approach and the appearance of this theatre is a quality that Italo Calvino defines as a *thoughtful lightness*, a notion that suggests to me both a gravity and a buoyancy: a capacity to take things seriously without losing a sense of being playful. I want to thoughtfully—lightly—interrogate, search and re-search the theatre. I want to ask some simple questions: ask what it takes to make it, ask why we might make it, and ask how we might make it, ask why and where the work happens and ask what can happen from it.

Jill Dolan has written that the theatre is capable of; "[...] small but profound moments in which performance calls the attention of the audience in a way that lifts everyone slightly above the present". Like her, I also want the theatre to be a vessel for some radical ideas, but I want to take a different, perhaps more pragmatic approach. I think I'm looking to find and create some methods for a theatre to lift us not above but into the present. Both *all that is solid melts into air* and *commonwealth* are attempts to examine ideas of both the theatre—and our—capacity and potential within—and after—its fact. They appear in social contexts where concepts of collective action can sometimes be difficult to imagine. In a place where we know there are things to be done, but we don't always know just what we can do.

The landscape of theatre in which they appear is also one filled with ideas and discussions around participation and interaction, a landscape where practices are often exploring new and exciting methods and where boundaries are often challenged. These activities illuminate an important aspect of dematerialized theatre, which chooses to see the act of sitting and listening in a room not as one of passive consumption, but also a form of participation.

I don't think of these pieces of work as solo performances, but instead as collaborations with an audience. I hope the words that I choose to use and the conditions they can help me to create can somehow allow an act of dialogue or *thinking together*. Though it may be me that's talking and the audience that is sitting and listening, I hope that they will recognize the importance of their role, as I hope you might as you read this now. I hope that whatever they (and you) are doing, we might think of everyone as actors all of the time. We all turn up to the theatre. We are all in the same room. We arrive at a place that I think and hope still has the potential to be a social environment, a place where we can describe who we are to each other, and where we can take some time to think about what we have got.

I want to use the theatre to open space and hold it open. Create opportunities that I think the rooms we call theatres can afford us. To take a chance to just apply the brakes a little and see where we are, to think about matters and think about what matters. And to ask the question: *what can we do?*

Andy Smith has been making theatre under the name a smith since 2003. His most recent solo works are *all that is solid melts into air* and *commonwealth*. Along with Karl James he is the co-director of *An Oak Tree, ENGLAND, The Author* and *Adler & Gibb* by Tim Crouch. Together, they were commissioned to write and perform a new work for The Almeida Theatre with the title *what happens to the hope at the end of the evening*.

CONSIDERING IMAGINATION

Katie Pearl

As a member of a community that makes, sells, sees, and administrates theater, I'm curious about the quality of time we are spending together. Of course each project, institution, and collaborator is different and our experiences vary radically. Yet I do I feel I can safely make some generalizations about ourselves as a field, and one of them pertains to our relationship to innovation. Here it is, and it will be no surprise to anyone: We value it. We are pushed, and push ourselves, to innovate. Do something new. Put a new spin on things. Solve a problem or situation in a new way. Being derivative is anathema. Innovate! Be original!

This book's editor asked us to consider innovation, and I'd like to do so by questioning the love affair we have with it. Not because I don't believe innovation is important, because I do. I question it because I'm not sure it has a solid foundation. I am concerned that the American Theater requires itself to be innovative without successfully supporting and nurturing its own imagination. A few years ago I encountered a book called *Imagination First*, co-authored by Scott Noppe-Brandon (the former executive director of the Lincoln Center Institute). It points out that in our society "(t)he general assumption is that the will to act must precede imagination—that you decide to do something before you imagine what it is. The reality is that imagination comes first... Until and unless we have the emotional and intellectual capacity to conceive of what does not exist, there is nothing towards which we are to direct our will and our resources" (San Francisco, Wiley and Sons, 2009; p8).

I believe that we, as theater makers and theater workers, know intuitively that we must "imagine first." We know that our creative process must begin with time to dream deeply, to get to know our inner voice, to listen for our impulses and urges, and to imagine and experiment with their possible forms—all this before the practical innovation, the actual making, can begin. But is the culture of American theater set up for that? As an artist or arts administrator, do you feel like there is, in the field as a whole or within your own particular institution or collaborations, time for your imagination to live? Is there room for it to grow? To find itself? To be expressed?

Is finding the time and space to imagine first a value that we share? Based in the many conversations I've had over the years with colleagues about our shared desire for more time and space to dream and to experiment, I'd say it is. Yet these same conversations indicate that while it's a value we share, it's not a value that we as a field are successful at prioritizing. I think there is often a block when it comes to prioritizing the cultivation of the imagination of theater artists. Not in our desire to do so, but in our effectiveness at ensuring that it happens. And if there is indeed this schism between what we value and what we make a habit of giving ourselves, the first step in figuring out how to close that gap is to recognize that it's there.

It is spring, 2006. I am subletting on the Upper West Side, in NYC to work on a new play with my collaborator Lisa D'Amour. It is morning, and I'm drinking my coffee, turning on my computer to read how it's going for my friends and colleagues at the Humana Festival. I go to the *New York Times* website, find Charles Isherwood's festival wrap-up, and read this: "There's not much point in aiming high if you can't hit your target. And is it really necessary for playwrights to dream up new worlds?" (April 5, 2006).

Now, I know this is old news. I turn back to it now only because it is an important example of our predicament, which shows up here as a kind of blindness towards the value of the theater artist's imagination. Over the years, Isherwood has consistently expressed his position on new writing, favoring work that hones more closely to realism over that which experiments with form or content. A concern I have for our field is the way in which this opinion has an impact not only on the kind of work that is being produced and supported by our major theaters, but also on the quality of time we are spending together as a community. I feel that it squelches our impulse to turn towards each other for imagination, experimentation, and innovation—and influences us instead to do our creative work within the safer bounds of what is tested and known to succeed (at least in the eyes of the *New York Times*). A *Times* review has long mattered disproportionately in our field—a bad review can both hurt a show and handicap a career. But as arts desks continue to get cut from news organizations around the country and the national critical discourse shrinks, the views expressed in the *New York Times* take on even more power. Because the *New York Times* remains the main arbiter for taste in our field, the mindset it represents becomes embedded in the national system that is evaluating our work. This evaluation teaches and influences audiences, administrators, and artists what our work should be—if we want it to be commercially viable.

To return to his quote above, I recognize that Isherwood might simply be trying to say there is mystery worth exploring in normal day-to-day life... and I do agree with him about that. But he is also making a significant condemnation of our writers' love affair with innovation, seemingly because he felt that we, as a field, were failing at it. This I don't agree with. The assertion that we shouldn't bother to imagine if it leads to failed innovation is both a stupid and dangerous stance—not just to our art form, but to our country as a whole. It is so obviously stupid and dangerous, one can't help but wonder how this blindness took hold? How did it manage to make it into the newspaper that is most influential to our field?

When I dig down just a little to explore the origins of this blindness, it quickly becomes impossible to extricate the field of American Theater from the field of American socio-economic values. Our blindness as a field has its roots in the national context of supply and demand in which our work takes part. We feel it daily: in order to do our work, we have to sell it; in order to sell it, we have to fit it into the packages that the buyer wants. So the pressure is great to conform to the demand—or at least to what we perceive the demand to be (a perception significantly tempered by reviews).

To be overly simplistic, in our system the focus is on the market—on objects that can be sold. So, as artists, we have gotten used to thinking that our value is attached to our objects: our plays, either as scripts or as productions. That is our capital. That is how we participate in this free market system. We could think of Isherwood-the-critic as merely a representative of our capitalist system who encourages the American Theater to think of ourselves as a big department store selling productions. And as our business coach, he only wants us to succeed. He only wants us to make sure our products are competitive enough to win the contest of getting people to buy tickets to see it. He only wants us *not* to put our works on the rack unless we're sure of their success. Unfortunately, in our market economy, that often means pushing out a product that attempts to stand out by being innovative, while sacrificing the quality of our experience making that product. In fact, Isherwood's commentary reveals himself less as the origin of our field's block against prioritizing imagination, and more as a victim himself: of a blindness caused by the capitalist system in which we all take part.

I was fortunate enough to be at a NET Microfest with Michael Rhod earlier this year, and heard him express his views on the market value of the artist. Michael's argument is that our capital as artists is not our product but our process. I will put a finer point on it and say it is our imagination. That is how we serve the world—by building a close relationship with our imaginations, by learning how to be in relationship to it, converse with it, articulate it, share it. We use it to see possibilities and make new paths. We use it to make new connections—which sometimes lead to wonderful aesthetic moments, other times to new integrations of art and social justice, other times to transformative experiences between artists and their communities. I'm not interested in ignoring to the system we are in—capitalist, materialist— but I'm very interested in a perception shift that will allow us to place proper value on our imaginations, and close the gap between what we know and what we do.

One way to achieve this perception shift is to move towards a view often expressed by Erik Ehn in the classes he teaches at Brown University: that we think of our performance as the accident of our rehearsal. To say "the performance is the accident of my rehearsal" requires that we believe that the process of imagining is actually more important than the success of the innovation. This is not the same thing as letting go of rigor and aesthetic standards. It is rather a re-focusing of values towards the process of making rather than towards a guarantee of product; it allows for an intentionality to that process, recognizing that if care is put into the making, the resulting product will "accidentally" reflect that care.

Another way I have found to achieve the perception shift is to move the center of my art making away from New York and out of the regional theater matrix. There are many environments where imagination is both valued and supported—my long-time creative home of Austin is the example I know best, and I feel it also in cities like New Orleans and Minneapolis. These towns have become known as "centers for new work," and while it is clear that they are communities where the imagination and experimentation is both prioritized and preferred, it would take another essay to satisfactorily examine the reasons *why* they have become that (though some good starting points might be the tenor of the local critical discourse, and the relative impossibility of supporting oneself in these smaller cities as a theater maker).

Finally, Erik Ehn also frequently says that "how we make something is what we mean." My understanding of his comment is that the way you get to something reveals its truest meaning. If you design a beautiful building but have it built with slave labor, it's an ugly building. If your family is nice and polite at the dinner table but you beat them to get them to be that way, you don't have a successful family. So my last query is this: if a product, a play, successfully sells but was developed in paucity and rehearsed on a constricted schedule with a stressed out, over-worked, under-paid creative team and administrative staff, can we really consider ourselves to be successful? Can we really consider it to be a successful play?

The performance demonstrates the quality of time we spend together. More obviously, the time we spend together demonstrates the quality of the performance. Whichever direction it goes, I am looking for a quality of performance and a quality of life, both; I am looking to increase the likelihood of having better accidents by paying more attention to my rehearsals... whether that's actual production rehearsals, or creative development time, or conversations with strangers, or the way I am with others within our field: listening to, nurturing, and fostering each other's growth. Ultimately, I dream that we can feel the American Theater around us and among us less as a store selling productions and more as an invitation to artists, administrators, and audiences to build a closer, more rigorous relationship with our own imaginations.

Katie Pearl is co-Artistic Director of PearlDamour, an OBIE Award-winning multidisciplinary performance making company she shares with Lisa D'Amour. As PearlDamour, Katie is a MAP and Creative Capital funded artist, and received the 2012 Lee Reynolds Award from the League of Professional Theater Women, given annually to a woman whose work for, in, about, or through the medium of theatre has helped to illuminate the possibilities for social, cultural, or political change.

TOWARDS A SLOW THEATRE

Lisa Schlesinger

The Kitchen Table

I first imagined a Slow Theatre Movement at my kitchen table. The table is hand built with two 17-inch wide walnut boards cut from the same local tree by my friend at Trappist Caskets. It took a long time for that tree to grow. I sometimes wonder if the table knows it might have been a casket. Now, there's bread on it and people around it. Now, a meal and the beginning of a conversation that turns into the beginning of a play, the beginning of a theatre. Everything I've ever thought of has been thought of before but it seems that at this moment in history the world needs to return to some simpler ways of doing things. An acoustic and manual revolution. And it's time to reclaim time.

Chekhov wrote that the task of a writer is to ask the questions, not answer them. Todd London has brilliantly stated some of the problems of American theatre in his books and articles of recent years from his vantage point at the center of new play development and theatre culture. Where do we find or how do we make solutions?

When I am puzzling over something, I remember Buckminster Fuller's famous quote:

> *"When I am working on a problem, I never think about beauty but when I have finished, if the solution is not beautiful, I know it is wrong."*

> *Work towards beautiful solutions.*

Sleeping Weazel

In 2011, in Boston, Charlotte Meehan re-activated her theatre company, **Sleeping Weazel**, originally founded in downtown Manhattan with her late husband, experimental filmmaker, David Hopkins. In its current formation, the company's mission reads:

*Sleeping Weazel produces plays and other theatrical events in a
variety of live venues and online. As a group of affiliated theatre,
visual, and performing artists, we are dedicated to presenting
curated mixed performance evenings as well as full productions
of individual work. We present leading-edge theatre locally,
and through month-long video exhibitions in our cyber art
gallery. We aim to cultivate the broadest possible audience base
through presenting works created by artists collaborating across
generations, cultures, and genres.*

The mission statement ends with an invitation:

*We invite you to join us in shared vision of surprise, spontaneity,
and discovery.*

In its first year, Sleeping Weazel highlighted the works of Caridad
Svich, Ruth Margraff, Suzanne Bocanegra, Lauren Kelley, Magdalena
Gomez, Robbie McCauley, Reverend Billy and others on stage and
in their cyber art gallery; enacted the Women in Action Festival,
and showcased works of the next generation of new writers. Ken
Prestininzi's Birth Breath Bride Elizabeth was among their first
productions. It moved to ArtsEmerson's The Next Thing Festival and
received rave reviews. The company, now in its third year, with a string
of successful productions and on-line exhibits, continues to produce
exciting new work off the radar.

Model what you want to be.

Tulips and Peppers

Slow Food movement is part of a global movement committed to a more
humane and environmentally sound approach to food, community, and
the world. Founder Carlo Petrini writes about the day in 1996 he turned
off a big-box store lined highway in Italy to eat at one of the many fine
restaurants tucked away in the agricultural region it crossed.

He ordered peperonata, the famous dish made from the locally grown
peppers of Asti. The dish arrived. It looked beautiful, but was tasteless.
The chef, his friend, explained that the peppers were now imported

from Holland. Each box contained 32 uniform and identical hybrid peppers perfect for export. Their colors were visually stunning and grown more cheaply because of intensive farming methods. Ironically, in what were once the pepper fields they now grew uniform tulip bulbs to export to Holland. The Slow Food movement started what is now a global movement towards a "slower" approach to many aspects of modern life. These include: slow education, money, sex, work, and exercise. What about a slow theatre? What might that look like?

Fuck uniformity, commercial industry standards and brands. Let's have our dirt and our desire and our taste back.

Theatre Oobleck

No director. New works. Free if you're broke. Twenty-seven years.

Theater Oobleck is a 27-year-old Chicago-based company that changes the rules of engagement in theatre. Their work has received critical acclaim locally, nationally and internationally. In recent years several productions have moved from Chicago to New York for successful off-Broadway runs.

On the company's website it says:

Oobleck has launched 70 productions of idiosyncratic new works, all created and developed by members of the ensemble, working in concert to create a collective vision without an overseeing director.

They have, in fact, no directors. No artistic director. No managing director. None. They quote from an unknown source:

Putting the burden of innovation on the director is like putting the prime minister in charge of the revolution, for the director, insofar as he remains a director, cannot help but defend that kind of theater in which he has a place of importance, suppressing those ancient models of the theater which do not require his services.

The company's primary goal is "to empower ourselves as individuals and as a collective." And because the company invites its audiences in to engage with and change the play while it is in process, they also empower their public.

Audience as company.

On Bread

The playwright, novelist, and scholar, Andras Nagy, drove around Budapest with a half loaf of bread on the ledge of the back seat of his car.

Isn't it stale? I asked.

Yes, he said. *But anyone who lived through the war would never throw away bread.*

What will we use it for, I asked.

Whatever we need it for, he answered.

While I was at the Iowa Playwrights' Workshop completing my MFA, I applied for a job baking bread at the co-op, a good way to support playwriting, I thought. *What bread baking experience do you have?* They asked in the interview. Yes, interview.

I learned to bake bread in the village square in Mardati, Crete. Baking was a multi-day affair. They fed the starter, collected wood, fired up the communal oven, mixed the dough in a stone trough, and shaped it on an old construction board. When the first set of loaves came out of the oven, we ate fat slices with butter and olives.

At the co-op the artesian bread was copyrighted. They had to pay a licensing fee. And it cost $4 a loaf! Only in the United States would we copyright something as essential as bread and turn it into a luxury item.

Now, I am back in Iowa teaching playwriting and I bake bread at home. Some years back, Mark Bittman published an adapted version of

Jim Lahey's recipe for No Knead bread in the New York Times under the title *The Secret of Great Bread: Let Time Do the Work.*

Here is my bread recipe, slightly altered, again:

3 cups flour (mixed grains)
1/4 - 1/2 tsp. yeast
1 1/2 tsp. salt
1 1/3 c water

Mix. Let rise, covered, 12-24 hours, depending on the season. Shape and cover for two hours in a tea towel for the second rise. I've lengthened the rise time because my process is slow. I seem to need more time than other people for just about everything.

Heat the Dutch oven at 450 degrees 1/2 an hour before you are ready to bake. Or find a friend with a brick oven. Or build one. Bake your bread, break it, eat it.

Making bread is simple, cheap, and fun. Every step of the process parallels the playwriting process. In fact, *ingredients* are used in the *bakeoff,* the first playwriting exercise of the year at Iowa. Like Lahey's bread recipe, this exercise was started by a master playwright at another program, probably changed when it was passed on. Or perhaps this is a rumor, like one that starts among people baking bread in the village square. And maybe, just maybe, the bread remembers its old world self. Most importantly,

Share bread and recipes. Pay what you can. Pass it on.

Bread and Puppet Theater

Bread and Puppet Theater was founded in 1963 in downtown Manhattan as a bread baker's theatre. It is one of the oldest, self-supporting, non-profit theatre companies in the country. In an excerpt of Peter Schumann's 50th anniversary letter he writes:

Bread and Puppet is based on bread baking and the not-for-sale distribution of bread at moments created by art, and these

moments are created in opposition to capitalist culture and habit. Therefore the puppet show is not only a puppet show, but an eating-bread-together event. We ask our hosts not only for performing space, but also for 400 bricks, fire wood, and fire permits to build and use itinerant bread ovens as part of our productions. From the beginning of the Bread and Puppet enterprises we decided to make two types of shows: inside shows meant for the viewers inside, and outside shows for the unrelenting political street. Both types of shows address the urgencies of the day as they come upon us.

Peter creates work as if the world were ending; he was born in Silesia and was a child during World War II. He creates monuments to life, to beauty, to possibility. Brilliantly. Constantly. He is a whirling dervish of theatre making. He's proof that "slow" does not necessarily mean slow. What it really means is authenticity. Creating an artistic aesthetic through practice and, in that process, creating an aesthetic for one's life, too.

Still, the Bread and Puppet performances allow the public to slow down. A circus in a field, a performance in a barn or in a church on the upper west side of Manhattan. At the end of a processional a great sun goddess puppet comes up over a hill. And always, the puppeteers offer bread. A sacrament.

The world is made sacred again.

How do you live?

I ask every artist I meet *how do you live?* How do you pay grocery bills, and make theatre, music, art, too? I believe we owe it to each other, and to the next generations, to be honest about this. So many of us are also teachers, housepainters, bread bakers. Some of us have patrons or trust funds. Some of us are broke. What are the "urgencies of the day"? How do we keep making art in an economy that supports commerce but does not speak honestly or openly about money? How do we keep hope?

How do you live?

What is a Slow Theatre?

Slow theatre is a way of making theatre and a way of living. It's not necessarily slow but it does allow time to do its work.

What's the difference between slow theatre and theatre? Time and resources.

In the commercial world, time equals money but in a creative world time equals possibility. Expansive and expanding realms of imagination to be shared and passed.

How do we give people time? How do we share wealth and experience? How do we support the new and unfamiliar? How do we break through old structures, borders, territories? How do we go beyond what we imagined for ourselves and for each other? How do we lift up those who can't go on any longer? How do we give what we most need?

Maybe we can start with bread.

Lisa Schlesinger is a playwright/theatre activist. A recipient of the NEA/TCG Playwrights Residency Award, the BBC International Playwriting Award, and a nominee for a USArtists Fellowship, her work is produced in the U.S. and internationally and published in *American Theatre* Magazine, *Performing Arts Journal*, and the *New York Times*.

COOKING OIL

Deborah Asiimwe and Emily Mendelsohn

The ghost of a teenage girl who sold aid illegally at the side of her village road asks a development worker *do you see me?* The girl and her death were invisible in the enormity of forces that dictate distribution of the world's resources. Her question lies at the heart of *Cooking Oil*, a new play and international collaboration (written by Deborah Asiimwe, directed by Emily Mendelsohn) exploring complex justice and the power dynamics embedded in the foreign aid industry.

Being asked to see or to be seen is a frightening thing. It is an invitation to be exposed, to be examined and to be judged. At a very human level, we have created a world of looking but not "seeing." Every day, we move from one place to another, and in our movements, we encounter people, we encounter situations, and we find ourselves either looking away or looking but not really seeing. We avoid eye contact with those we don't know, we are afraid to see, and to be seen. Even when we are compelled to "see," it is likely that we will do so from a "safe" standpoint so as to preserve ourselves from the real commitment of "seeing." Maria in *Cooking Oil* asks us this question at different moments of her life, *"Do you see me?"* What does it feel like to be looked at, but not really seen?

We met as graduate students at CalArts in 2006; developed work together; traveled together on Erik Ehn's trips to East Africa studying art's capacity to participate in acts of healing and developing pedagogical models based on mutuality. *The Cooking Oil* project comes out of this network and thinking. Together we teach our ears to "see" by intensely listening to one another with compassion, to hear what is said and unsaid, we teach our bodies to "see" by intensely feeling the unspoken, that which can only be communicated by a movement, a gesture, a facial expression, a breath. We have been creating spaces of "seeing" not only with our eyes, but with our entire being. Sometimes, with multiple languages spoken in the rehearsal room, "seeing" becomes less of a choice but an obligation. We feel uncomfortable "seeing" someone struggling to express themselves in the spoken language, our bodies shift uncomfortably because they are reminding us of the need to "see" and to be "seen" sometimes in our most uncomfortable elements.

In looking at ways to stage the question, we create an obstacle for literal representation, and the work has become more visually spare, more focused on aural entry points—layered music, text, breath to create world. In the play, characters wander in and out of each other's dreams, and earnestly negotiate a shared reality. Production designer Shannon Scrofano and costume designer Stella Atal work with varied artifacts—empty cans donated from the World Food Programme (WFP), bark cloth fabric, T-shirts donated to Africa and sold at market, a computer, cassava. Our world is not the intersection of static cultures, but an invocation built out of materials in tension: traditional/modern, Western/African, home-made/manufactured, individual/collective. Objects/artifacts/practices/songs/stories/languages all serve as tools to make Maria—her struggles, her dreams, her—visible.

I would say that ours is a process of construction and deconstruction and construction and deconstruction and construction: and purposeful impulses, following intuition that translates into technique, finding language of what it is that we are creating, a room of collisions, of conceptualizing and of allowing our bodies to articulate what it is that we have conceptualized, of letting our bodies and what they have internalized be challenged, and be asked to shift again, and try something new, something different. Coming to what we believe in as a process, not so much of reasoning, but of removing obstacle.

The style within which the text is written is informed by an art of storytelling in the Kinyankore culture where the storyteller invites her/ his listeners on a journey with her/him. It is an invitation to participate, to directly experience with the person leading the journey. The voice of the storyteller may be singular, but the act of invitation turns the singular voice into a communal and a collective one. The story becomes a shared dream and/or reality, it becomes communally owned, the storyteller and the listener become one, the space of separation gets blurred, together you "see," together you are "seen."

At its best, the project strives to perform a tiny-scale interruption of patronizing ways of thinking about aid, and the hope becomes that out of interruption might follow questions, new relationships, the work of reorienting. How do we imagine change in a world that includes us?

Cooking Oil performed at the ATX/ Arts+Innovation Complex Warehouse June 6-9, 2013 produced by Los Angeles Performance Practice in association with the CalArts Center for New Performance, and was supported in part by the City of Los Angeles, Department of Cultural Affairs.

Deborah Asiimwe is a playwright, producer and performer from Uganda. Her plays have received productions and readings in the US and East Africa. Asiimwe received her MFA in Writing for Performance from CalArts and was the overall winner of the 2010 BBC World Service African Performance playwriting competition.

Emily Mendelsohn is an American director. Recent work includes a Ugandan/American *Maria Kizito* (Erik Ehn) with ArtSpot Productions, and the American premiere of *Children of Killers* (Katori Hall). She received an MFA in Directing from CalArts, and a 2010 Fulbright Fellowship to Uganda.

BACKWARD COUNTRY

Elaine Avila

December 2010. I am asked to fly to Nanjing to deliver a series of lectures on American and Canadian playwrights from 1970-2010. A professor and his graduate students are preparing the first book on the subject ever published in China. When I arrive, my energetic, knowledgeable host asks me a question, which is more of a statement, "you must think China a very backward country."

We were traversing two of the most staggeringly huge cities on the planet, Nanjing and Shanghai, a commute involving two vast hyper modern subway networks, a high speed train, and a brisk cab ride to where I would be staying—the "Nanjing Expert Hotel" on the charming, garden like campus of Nanjing Normal University.

I was stunned by his question. Did I find China backward? No. Was he hoping I would compliment him on the modernity of Chinese cities? I did. In my sleep deprived state, I managed to say something about how impressed I was by the depth and breadth of Chinese history, and the opportunity to ride one of the fastest trains in the world, from Shanghai to Nanjing. My answer was honest but careful. In China, discussing innovation and backwardness are politically dangerous topics.

Immediately before I left for China, Liu Xiaobo was awarded the Nobel Peace Prize "for his long and non-violent struggle for fundamental human rights in China," but the Chinese government did not let him out of jail to attend the ceremony. Visual artist/activist Ai Wei Wei had been beat up and detained by Chinese authorities, his blog has been shut down, his studio bulldozed. One of his pieces commemorates the lives of thousands of children who died in the Sichuan earthquake of 2008, due to shoddy construction of their school. For his show in Munich, Germany, Ai Wei Wei made a piece out of 9000 children's backpacks spelling out "she lived happily for seven years in this world," a quote from one of the mothers who lost her child. (See Alison Klayman's documentary, "Ai Wei Wei: Never Sorry.") Given the dangers my Chinese colleagues and the students were facing, I let them broach the subject of China's contemporary politics and policies.

I trusted them to assess their own risks.

Yet these topics—innovation, and backwardness, were essential for us to consider. Together, the United States and China account for 40 percent of the world's greenhouse gases. Canada pulled out of the Kyoto protocol on climate change. Due to global warming, Shanghai/Nanjing/Beijing are becoming unbearably hot in the summers, and Shanghai is beginning to sink. Everywhere we went, people were wearing surgical facemasks, some with "Hello Kitty" or checkerboard designs on them. This practice, initially to prevent the spread of colds, has been expanded to include avoiding sickness due to air pollution.

Where did my host's question about being backward come from? At a banquet a group of male professors kindly held in my honor, some addressed the passion for progress. These professors were all peasants who had been supported in becoming academics, under Mao. One of the professors said, "if you have starved in your youth, you can never make enough money." Later, I learned that this remark likely had to do with how much rural people suffered during the Great Leap Forward (1958-1961), which these professors would have certainly endured in their youth.

Suddenly the word "backward" became clear. My grandparents were also peasants. My grandfather immigrated to North America, from rural Portugal, in search of an education. Backward is a word that implies that someone does not know how to behave in the city, at court, at university. It is a word that hangs over every action of an immigrant family that is trying to get access to education and better paying jobs— you dress, speak, and move to fit in. Yet innovation, fitting in, moving forward have brought us to environmental and cultural crisis. I'm not only talking about climate change, but about language loss. According to anthropologist Wade Davis, we are due to lose 50% of our planet's 7,000 indigenous languages in the next 100 years. This is a frightening loss of story, culture, animal, planet, and ancestral knowledge.

My topic, American/Canadian Playwrights from 1970-today, made me literally look backward. It became a subject we were all free to explore, a way to discuss everything. My topic surprised me. In Canada and the U.S., I am regularly asked to speak to our problems—our lack of gender parity, the dearth of stories that reflect our actual communities on stage. Preparing my lectures for China showed me our story could also be considered a successful battle for free speech, theatres' positive impact on social policy, and the inclusion of writers from many cultures and gender perspectives.

I began my lectures by exploring two moments that made me want to be a playwright. The first moment was remembering when Sam Shepard was the playwright-in-residence at San Francisco's Magic Theatre. Many of us who grew up in the San Francisco Bay Area at that time loved his wild adventurous writing. It made us feel we could do, say anything. My research quickly reminded me his wildness was hard won. The Magic's writer-in- residence immediately before Shepard was Michael McClure, who was arrested along with his cast for putting on his play, *The Beard*. McClure was made an example of in the ongoing fight for free speech involving Lenny Bruce, Allen Ginsberg's *Howl* and the San Francisco Mime Troupe.

The second moment that inspired me to be a playwright was seeing Emily Mann's *Execution of Justice* at San Jose Repertory Company, a play commissioned and created by the Eureka Theater, chronicling Dan White's trial for his assassination of San Francisco City Supervisor Harvey Milk (the first openly gay person to be elected to public office in California) and San Francisco Mayor George Moscone. The play put the community on trial.

In our tradition, we have many plays that have affected social policy, from John Herbert's *Fortune and Men's Eyes* (one of the most produced Canadian plays, which influenced prison reform and raised awareness of gay rights) to *The Lamarie Project*. Tim Miller, Holly Hughes, Karen Finley, John Fleck (the NEA 4) continue to fight for free speech, gay rights and funding of the arts in America. Canadian Métis Marie Clements' *The Unnatural and Accidental Women* tells the stories of murdered Aboriginal women, and seeks redress for how these murders were ignored, deemed "unnatural and accidental." We have a powerful history of the theatre being a place for social debate and political change. The movements of the seventies to include writers from many cultural backgrounds and gender identities may have been imperfect, but they have yielded results. Since 2000, two African American women (Suzan-Lori Parks, Lynn Nottage) and two Latino/as (Nilo Cruz, Quiara Alegría Hudes) have won the Pulitzer Prize.

The professor who was hosting me supervised a cadre of all female graduate students, each in charge of a chapter on a different playwright, from Fornes to Kushner. These women were filled with passionate questions and enthusiasm. They were the hope of their families, the first to get to university degrees, from diverse, rural villages. They took me through the Nanjing Place, to Purple Mountain. We had deep discussions about Chinese and English Literature, Chinese history, and their future plans. Resonant, symbolic gifts were exchanged. They asked, "Is Wendy Wasserstein a feminist?" I asked, "Is your mother a feminist?" They laughed and told me many stories about the role of women in China. For example, female PhDs and Professors are sometimes called a "third gender," because some believe they would not make good wives.

I was asked to speak throughout Nanjing. After these lectures, I was asked:

—In China, strangers are bad. Why does Blanche in *A Streetcar Named Desire* depend on their kindness? Aren't strangers bad in America?

—In *The Glass Menagerie*, why doesn't Laura listen to her mother? In China, we listen to our parents.

I began to re-examine our own stories. I had a new admiration for the way our "family plays" critique the effects of capitalism, the weight of history, slavery, and war on individuals. But I also began to wonder. What happens when you're old enough to play Amanda instead of Laura? Is overthrowing the parents always good?

And I began to reclaim the words "Backward Country." I didn't want to lose 50% of the languages on our planet. When I returned from China, I began working with the oldest stories I could find. I collaborated with Inuit storyteller Arvaarluk (Michael) Kusugak on a new show for Pangaea Arts. Arvaarluk's stories contain powerful metaphors about the dangers of selfishness and cruel behavior, a reverence for the sea as the source of food and life. Some lines in the stories might even be 1000 years old, and the meanings of the stories are told, contemplated, debated from Alaska to Greenland. Arvaarluk inspires many to look backward, into their own ancestry and connection to the land and story. I have begun a series of plays inspired by my

Portuguese heritage—*Lost and Found in Fado* (supported by the British Columbia Arts Council), *Kitimat* (Recipient, Mellon Elemental Arts Commission, Pomona College), and *Café A Brasileira* (Winner, Disquiet International Play Award).

Reflecting on our history since 1970, connecting with these students and faculty in China made me realize—innovation isn't always good, being backward isn't always bad.

Elaine Avila is a Canadian/American playwright of Portuguese descent. She is currently Playwright in Residence at Pomona College and the Playwrights Theatre Centre. Awards: Disquiet International Play Award, Lisbon; Best New Play, Victoria Critics' Circle, Canada; Audience Favorite, Festival de Cocos, Panama. Her collected plays are available at NoPassport Press.

THE AUDIENCE: FRIEND, FOE OR INNOCENT BYSTANDER?

QUESTIONS ABOUT THE INTERSECTION OF ART AND COMMUNITY

Leila Buck

I think a lot about the audience when I write.
In fact, I'm thinking about you right now.
Well maybe not you specifically, but my ideas of who you might be.
What made you start reading this?
Do you like me—I mean, my blog post—so far?
Will you keep reading? Why or why not?
Do you prefer wit or sincerity? (I can do both, I swear.)
How much should I base what I say about audiences on what I think may or may not interest you?

I'm also wondering:
Will you judge me if I use "they" instead of "it" when referring to the audience? Do I need to prove that I understand it's a singular noun but really it refers to a group of people and I don't like talking about people as "it"?
And come to think of it, doesn't that say a lot about our dilemma with audiences (did you see how I snuck in the plural there to avoid the whole it/they thing?):
When should we treat our audience as an "it"—an object or recipient of our work, and when a "them"—a group of living, breathing beings whose active participation in that work makes it possible?

Which brings me to the real questions on my mind right now:
How do we stay true to our own voice(s) in creating our work, and actively committed to engaging others in that process?
How can we engage not just the audience that comes to our shows, but the wider communities that rarely do?
Is it possible to remain committed to real community engagement without compromising our integrity or needs as professional artists—whatever they may be?

And what do our responses to these questions say about what we do and who we are?
You know—details.

My beliefs about the intersection of art and community are shaped by many years of training and work as a teaching artist based in the philosophies of Augusto Boal.
Boal saw and practiced theater as a "rehearsal for revolution". (Yes, I'm a lefty. Go figure.)
I won't try to describe his many processes here, as they are complex, and many of you, I'm sure, know them well. The elements of his work I think most relevant to this discussion are:
a) the use of theater as a space for exploring different responses to injustices or problems in our daily lives.
b) the role of audience members as "spectACTors" whose participation changes the course of the performance itself and sparks dialogue about how to move that change beyond the theatrical space and into their lives.

My own practice of these ideas has evolved over years of work with students and teachers of all ages in the NY public schools, followed by some burnout, some break time, and more years of teaching as a guest artist in a range of communities from here to Australia and back again.
The one thing that has emerged as constant for me through all this is the balance between owning that I have something unique to offer those gathered, and opening to what they have to share with me. And it is that same balance I find myself seeking in my creative work and process.

I began my writing career, as many actors do, by creating and touring a solo performance about my own life. I developed my commitment to the audience as partner through years of performing that work in community settings—universities, conferences, and cultural centers —even one high school auditorium back in the day, complete with bells going off mid-performance as bags were fetched from lockers.

Some of my best moments on stage and off occurred in shows and talkbacks from the International School of Beijing to Dickinson, South Dakota's second annual diversity conference.

My favorite aspect of these experiences was the opportunity to engage directly with the audience both during the show and afterwards. One blessing of performing one's own work is the chance to sense how your words are landing in the moment, and if you choose to, change them on the spot (much to the board operators' chagrin) to speak more directly to the energy of the people in the room.

After all, in solo performance your only partner out there IS your audience. And when it clicks, that connection is unlike any other. The vulnerability and honesty of sharing a deeply personal experience with a roomful of strangers can be profoundly beautiful, powerful, even—dare I say—spiritual.

To honor this connection, when I began developing my second full-length solo piece, IN THE CROSSING, I would make sure there was a discussion with the audience after every reading or performance. I wanted to know how the play was affecting people and have a chance to dialogue with them.

The story was a very personal one—about my experience with my husband in Lebanon during the 2006 Israeli-Hezbollah war—a subject about which, not surprisingly, many people have strong opinions.

In spite of my best efforts to include a range of voices and viewpoints—in particular the genuine warmth, humor and caring of my Jewish in-laws or Israeli friends—some audience members felt my story to be one-sided, biased, even irresponsible, and asked, suggested, or demanded that I alter it to include perspectives beyond my own.

Other audience members, and many friends and colleagues, even those who didn't necessarily share my political or personal opinions, would tell me to ignore those demands and stick to my own voice: "Just tell your story."

I soon realized that what I wanted, and needed, to do lay somewhere in between—and that the struggle to find that balance was both the conflict, and the heart, of my play.

So for the better part of three years, I experimented with ways of writing that journey into the piece.

I tried representing everything from voices in my head, to angry audience members literally interrupting what I had to say.

Many other voices helped me along the way: an incredible team of actors, Liz Frankel, the EWG, countless readings and conversations with generous artists and audiences far and wide, and the constant guidance and insight of my incredible director Shana Gold.

After a record number of drafts, we finally settled on a combination that felt like it worked.

But even with three other actors now representing multiple viewpoints, I soon realized it was impossible to write something that represented even a fraction of the many perspectives on "the Arab-Israeli conflict"—or for that matter, how they had shifted according to what happened in the world that day.

So since my audiences and collaborators had already helped shape so much of the play, I decided to let them do the rest of the work for me. I turned the second act into a staged talkback—partially scripted based on past audience responses—with built-in moments for audience members to ask questions, share responses, and challenge the actors in role, the play itself, and the political and personal issues it raises.

The result is part storytelling, part theater, part town hall, and part structured improvisation, and continues to evolve each time we perform. It's messy, and terrifying, and doesn't always fully work.

But I wouldn't trade it for anything.

Because it reminds me, every time, of what I love most about what we do—the thing that makes it so unique, and powerful, and bold:

The fact that performer and audience are in the same space, at the same time, together, sharing all the discomfort and danger, beauty and possibility of that interaction.

In the end, isn't it this very relationship with the audience, this sharing of space together that makes theater what it is?

I mean, if a tree falls and no one unwraps a candy...

Yet at times I have felt myself, and other theater artists, take a kind of pride or refuge in the inaccessibility of our art form; the idea that it is a loftier art because it is not a medium for the masses like our more mainstream competitors, film and TV.

Or we feel torn between catering too much to our audiences—producing more successful or lucrative but sometimes less fulfilling work—or too little, producing work we love that is not seen as widely, or paid as well.

Recently I've been excited to see more and more work experimenting with audiences in new, direct, provocative ways.

I'm also inspired by artists and companies who successfully balance their work in professional theatre with an ongoing engagement with students and communities.

But there remains a division between works created in community, outside the mainstream theatrical establishment, and those created and performed in more traditional or "professional" settings.

And in most work produced outside of community spaces, the audience's role is primarily in response to a story or experience, rather than actively shaping it.

So it seems then that the larger issue is not whether it is possible to truly engage our audiences in a fulfilling creative process that produces successful work.

It's how to convince both audiences and artists that there is something to be gained in doing so.

And from there, new(ish) questions arise:
Is it possible to approach communities of strangers not as audiences but "spectACTors"—integral parts of the creative process—and create work that will be seen beyond those communities?
By doing so might we expand those audiences themselves, forging new alliances with communities that do not otherwise feel connected to what we do?
Could making our audiences more active participants in our creative process help to broaden and deepen not only our connections to communities, but the relevance and immediacy of our entire art form?

I believe the answer to all these questions is yes. The challenge for me is HOW.

That one, I'm still working on—Most recently, thanks to a commission from Wesleyan University through the Doris Duke foundation's Building Bridges grant, to create a theatrical piece with students and community on the vast subject of Muslim women.

In that spirit, I'd love to hear your questions, ideas, and challenges in response to any of the above.

I hope this little post will be just one small part of a larger, ongoing conversation between us and beyond.

Leila Buck is an inter-cultural writer, performer, and teaching artist. Writing highlights: *In the Crossing* (Public, NYTW, Culture Project–WCS). Acting highlights: *Aftermath* (NYTW–Drama League nomination); *Scorched* (Wilma-Barrymore Award). Publication: *American Theatre*; *Etching Our Own Image: Voices from the Arab American Art Movement; Four Arab-American Plays.* Member: EWG-Public; Usual Suspect—NYTW.

BILLS, E-MOTIONS, MANIFESTOS

Saviana Stanescu

("Theatre that challenges and evokes emotion from its audience but also pays the bills.")

As our book's editor gracefully asked me to write something about innovation in theatre for the 2013 TCG National Conference blog salon and later for this book, a myriad of ideas started to overlap and fight for supremacy in my brain:

I should write an essay called "Challenging Aristotle: Brecht, Artaud, Grotowski, Sarah Kane."
"Representation versus Presentation."
"Slice of life versus power of imagination."
"Psychological realism versus post-modern deconstruction."
"The beauty and complexity of non-naturalistic plays."
"Cross-cultural interdisciplinary performance and the role of theatre in fostering social change."

Yes, I must bring up the need for a political theatre, for new plays that unequivocally address hot problems of our society: "Risk-taking thought-provoking topics in theatre and performance."

That's a major issue but I can't cover it in 1500 words.

I know: I ought to discuss plays by women and the multi-climax structure as opposed to the traditional "phallic" one in which dramatic events build towards the well-earned culmination. I could even shed some light on hefty dramas versus "light" comedies.

No, it's my responsibility as a Romanian-born NYU-trained playwright (dramatic writing and performance studies), who used to work as a theatre critic for a major newspaper back in Bucharest, to write about "innovation in context": what is considered innovative in continental Europe where a director-driven ensemble-based theatre culture is still prevalent and what is deemed innovative here in the US where the playwright's vision is often sacred. Theatricality as an intrinsic link to innovation? Collaboration and the end of *auteur*-directors? A more expansive understanding of *play*-writing?

Difficult questions. I better focus on the ways in which TV series are influencing theatre and acknowledge the sexiness of the episodic, cinematographic storylines.

No, what has to be said is that mid-career theatre artists need more support, they paid their dues and then some, it's high time to get them the recognition and appreciation they deserve and stimulate them to continue to grow and innovate. Yes, I must come up with a well-documented analysis of freelancers' hardships in a free-market consumerist theatre system as opposed to the state-subsidized one. The imperative of making profit versus the intellectual luxury of doing art for art's sake.

No, I have to talk about New York and New Work. Theatre has historically proven to be a powerful tool for cross-cultural dialogue and awareness raising. NYC, with its diverse population, is the perfect playground for such envelope-pushing performative endeavors.

However, when people talk about theatre in NYC, most of them think "Broadway!" while the less glamorous Off-Off Broadway and Off-Broadway are arguably the most innovative artistic 'hoods of the Big global Apple.

OK, I should use this opportunity to talk about my own work, after all my play *Waxing West* won the 2007 Innovative Theatre Award for Outstanding Full-Length Script. *Waxing West, Aliens with Extraordinary Skills, Ants, Lenin's Shoe*, and my other "American" plays explore hyphenated identities and the immigrant experience, trying to capture that unique in-between space where expatriates and their American dreams/nightmares dwell.

No, that's not necessarily the point to be made in a blog on innovation. Immigrant narratives are at home in the US. Or so we hope.

Yes, I should write about poetic non-linear plays, plot-less dramas, in-yer-face theatre, multi-media performance, hybrid theatre, inter-disciplinary shows, devised-theatre, docudramas, re-imagining the classics, site-specific experiences, audience-interaction, conceptual performance, dance-theatre, movement-theatre, poor theatre, environmental theatre, immersive theatre, post-dramatic theatre, contemporary performance...

And then, as I was grading my Ithaca College Theatre Arts students' manifestos, it dawned on me. I should let them talk. They are the voices of the future, the echo of "tomorrow". What makes them believe in theatre, what's innovative for them? The final assignment I gave to my "Contemporary Developments in Theatre&Performance" class was to write a one-page artistic manifesto, a compelling plea for a form of theatre they believe in and hope to make after graduation. I copy below a few excerpts from their texts. The students' manifestos give us some revelatory insights into the needs and dreams of the next generation of theatre makers—the ones carrying new "innovation seeds" in their backpacks, so let's take a peek inside:

Lucy Walker: *For a Civic Theatre*
Here's my wishlist, for what I hope and know theatre could do and be, which would still let everyone else do what they want to do with theatre.
I wish for:
—a theatre not of believability and naturalism, but of emotional authenticity which understands you don't need the exact fluffy rug from the exact historical moment to access the exact core of the material (basically everything Grotowski said about getting rid of all the junk hiding the performers)
—a theatre open to all sorts of genres and styles, encompassing total art under the umbrella of theatre, retaining the joy and spark of theatre while losing the creativity-stifling rules of pure art and the fourth wall; who says the living newspaper is done with?
—a theatre valuing humanity over plays, and process over product
—but yet, still a theatre in which art for art's sake is possible, and it is possible to be overwhelmed by visual, physical, emotional, spiritual, and intellectual beauty of a piece that just hits you and makes you suddenly understand something you did not before (...)

Kaylyn Syvret: *(...) Where are the new and innovative writers? I have to believe they are out there and are just not being given the chance to showcase their new works to a broader audience. Nowadays,* commercial theater, and even sometimes regional theater, is very focused on revivals of old classics. I understand that revivals have their place; they are recognizable, they sell tickets, put butts in seats and keep the finances of the theater world above water. However, as someone who loves theater, I still have to hope that other people, who truly love theater as well, will still come and see a new work simply for the sake of experiencing a new set of ideas, instead of just for the title.

Sam Gates: *There is obviously a gap growing and we, as theatre artists should be afraid. I know at first, this sounds pretty silly, but trust me that our art is on track for extinction. Like many other historic inventions throughout the history of mankind, we improve upon our previous achievements. From science to the a-track to basketball, we refine, we adapt, and we perfect an invention. Many people (outside of this class, of course) argue that theatre is one of these old inventions, which we have already improved upon with—the movie. Sure, you could say that theatre will be like books, still in existence and just less popular, but the costs associated with theatre continue and will continue to rise, while books can now be published electronically for free and distributed for a small fee. Same goes for radio and for film— electronic media at our fingertips that theatre is slowly losing the competition to. This is why my charge, my goal for theatre, is to help theatre evolve further into being an art form of integrated multimedia while telling the same complex, stimulating stories. This theatre is not too different from our theatre today—it just needs more integration of technology and greater accessibility. (...)*

Sara Stevens: *When I think about the theatrical world today, it is difficult not to think about my place within it, and in an ideal world that kind of theatre that I want to create. Right away I come to one definite conclusion, I would like to be a theatre artist in a world that seems to have a place for me. What I mean by that is I get so discouraged sometimes thinking about what my options are in terms of next year and the years to come. I feel extremely unlucky to have fallen in love with new work, work that captures an audience and forces them to think about a social issue, or work that is inspired by Artaud and Brecht, because I seem to get the idea that if I want to create this theatre I will never be able to create rent. Maybe I am wrong, and maybe this manifesto is supposed to be an uplifting piece* *about how passionate I am about theatre that gets in people's faces, makes a statement, challenges the art form as we know it, but I can't write that paper knowing that I will hopefully be getting a weekly 50 dollar stipend to maybe possibly get to observe other people making that kind of theatre (...) In conclusion, I like theatre that is challenging, that does more than entertain (although I certainly think there is a place for that kind of theatre) and my goal for the future is to find some way to not just make theatre that challenges and evokes emotion from its audience, but also pays my bills. Let's call that theatre, "Theatre that challenges and evokes emotion from its audience but also pays the bills."*

Saviana Stanescu is a playwright and scholar originally from Romania. Her plays include *Waxing West, Aliens with Extraordinary Skills, Ants* and *Useless*. Her works have been seen at LaMama, The Women's Project, NJ Rep, and theatres in Europe and Latin America. She co-edited the play anthologies *Romania After 2000* with Daniel Gerould and *Global Foreigners* with Carol Martin. Her English-language plays are published by Samuel French and NoPassport Press. She is an Assistant Professor in the Department of Theatre Arts at Ithaca College in New York.

ELIOT FORGOT
THE RELUCTANT VAMPIRES.

Ian Rowlands

Sarah Kane, in *Psychosis 4:48* places herself *"Last in a long line of literary kleptomaniacs (a time honoured tradition)"* thereby echoing T.S. Eliot who stated, *"Good writers borrow, great writers steal."* However I am uncertain as to whether Eliot had anything to say about writers who, not only steal ideas, but feast on the very souls and base emotions of their subjects (victims). I am such a vampire; a soul sucker, *"an emotional plagiarist, stealing other people's pain, and subsuming it into my own..."* (*Crave*)–though, it could be argued that Kane's main pre-occupation was with autolysis to the point of nothing... silence.

I guess, we all aim for silence, thankfully, for my family, I have gone beyond the impulse of aiming for nothing. As a consequence, I suck souls for a living. However, I am a soul sucker with a growing conscience. With each soul consumed, to feed my dramatic desire, pangs of guilt wrack me. And yet, I keep sucking and writing. What else can a reluctant vampire do? I leech the souls of others, appropriate their emotions and lives, and place them unashamedly in my own dramatic narratives (and in so doing, in the public domain). But, what right do I have to exploit the very being of others? "I am a writer," I claim. But, is that a defense? Increasingly this dilemma has led me to question my actions! And believe me, such self-doubt is not a good thing for a reluctant vampire!

Let me present a case study: *Fragments of Journeys Towards the Horizon.*

Form: a monologue.

Theme: an exploration of friendship and cross-cultural collaboration. (Sounds like slim pickings, but oh, how I feasted!)

Background: I met the Dutch writer/director, Jeroen van den Berg at The Lark, NY. We were both International Associates of that development company. Twice, our visits to that city coincided. Both times we bonded over sushi and Brooklyn Beer. Back in Europe we built upon our friendship—I visited Amsterdam, van den Berg visited my city. During each visit we would discuss collaboration; blood sharing! But, vampires are not natural collaborators. We are perverse beings who subvert the natural order; true collaboration is anathema, and yet we set out with the best intentions.

However, two years down the line, and despite sustained intent, our dreams of collaboration had amounted to nothing. Unfortunately, having previously received an R&D grant from Arts Council Wales, I needed to produce blood, and came under increasing pressure to deliver it.

Process as form: Lacking a shared vision, I used the very nature of our failed collaborative process as the basis for a narrative (a monologue which I hoped would spark van den Berg's own dramatic intervention). However, early on in the process, I began to feel that the narrative needed a juxtaposing strand with which to intertwine; lacking van den Berg's at the time.[5]

It was then that a dear friend from Ireland (a producer with whom I had collaborated several times over), died of cancer. The death of someone with whom I had collaborated extensively threw the then current impasse into broader relief. Placing my deceased friend both at the heart and the periphery of the text, *Fragments of Journeys Towards the Horizon* began to evolve into a deeper exploration of friendship. The Irish strand juxtaposed "cutely" with the Welsh/Dutch, somehow accentuating the presumptuous, fleeting and fragile nature of friendship. Below, the narrator/self recalls meeting van den Berg for the first time...

I stood, corner of fifty-sixth and eighth, outside The Vitamin Shop waiting for you. Yes, I waited for you! I am more empirical in time

---

[5] Since writing this article, both the Dutch Performing Fund and Arts Council Wales have financed a production of *Fragments of Journeys* towards the Horizon. By now, van den Berg's intervention has supplanted the Irish elements within the main body of the text and as a consequence, mutated it. Full production will be realized in Summer 2016.

*and place. You float through life like... like fucking Denver, outwards
from a virtual centre! What? Yeah, you float. Ok, that's how I imagine
you. I said, I imagine; choose to imagine, maybe. Ok, you don't float.
You appear to float... through life... it's just my perception, ok! You
probably perceive things of me. Do I censor them? Do I fuck! Will you
listen! Will you listen? You keep interrupting me, I'm trying to... God's
sake! Louder than a fucking train. Listen, (THEN CALMER) please...*

Soul as content: Three lives collide in *Fragments*—the lives of van
den Berg, my Irish friend and my own. The intertwining threads
were the actual journeys we had made together; in the case of van
den Berg, a walk around the island of Terschelling (NL), in the case
of my Irish friend, our last walk together when I carried him to his
grave in Galway (Ireland). And, though the journeys are placed in
mythic relief, the core dramatic narrative is truth; play as document/
testimony (inspired by Emily Mann's *Testimonies*—though obviously
Mann used testimony techniques to explore socio-political topics as
opposed to my work which explores the nature of work itself).

The precedent for this model was well established. Whilst on periodic
sabbatical in NY (between 2006 and 2009) I became increasingly
fascinated by the process of 'play reading', in its myriad forms. Following personal experience gained developing Desire Lines at The Lark
(later published and staged by Sherman Cymru *www.shermancymru.
co.uk*), I wanted to write a play about the reading of a play.

It seemed, and still seems to me (especially reading Todd London),
that the majority of plays written, and playwrights in the USA remain
stuck in the hell of "reading land"—so little potential reaches kinetic.[6]
Such depressing, fascinating waste.

As a starting point, Daniella Topol (the director with whom I eventually
collaborated upon that project), suggested that I write the "play within
the play" (as in, the play that is being read within the play about the
reading of that play), in its entirety. This could then be read by "real"
actors as if it was "the main gig" (as in, a stand-alone play without
a hidden agenda). Both reactions to this text and reflections upon

---

[6] See *Dramatic Entrapment in Reading Land*, CTR Backpages Vol 21

the process of reading itself, could then form the basis of the main narrative—the play about the reading of a play.[7]

Re-reading the above, even I'm reminded of Danny Kaye: "The pellet with the poison's in the vessel with the pestle; the chalice from the palace has the brew that is true!" Confused? "Bear with," as they say.

I reference the above as, one day, prior to a reading of *(A/The) Biography of a Thing* (the eventual title for the play about the reading of a play), I was taken aside by a practitioner who had participated in a reading of a previous draft. The practitioner stated that he/she had an "issue" with the latest draft (and when a New Yorker says he or she has an issue, you have a problem!). The practitioner believed that a tragic event recounted in the text, was a direct lift from his/her life; believing that he/she had shared the detail of that event with me in confidence. In truth, it was not the case. It was only after I had convinced the practitioner that it was based upon another person's (victim's) experience that the reading was allowed to begin. A vampire's life is one fraught with issues. Once a person knows of your vampire tendencies, issues abound; whether real or imagined. Can a vampire ever be trusted?

In *(A/The) Biography of a Thing*, two actresses know a writer called Bill (the fictitious author of *Troyanne*—the play within the play. Both are questioned about their relationship with Bill by Drew, an interviewer:

> *Drew Did the stuff he wrote about you, hurt you...*
> *personally?*
> *Molly Mmm... (she thinks)*
> *Anja (she thinks) ... did it hurt me*
> *personally?*
> *Drew If you don't want to answer that...*
> *Molly No, just thinking about it...*

> *MOLLY AND ANJA ECHO EACH OTHER/DOVE TAIL ENDS*
> *OF LINES*

---

[7] *Historia*, plays by Ian Rowlands has recently been published by No Passport Press ISBN 978-1-312-71497-7.

Anja ... just thinking...
Molly If I was honest,...
Anja ... honestly...
Molly ...then I'd have to say....
Anja Yes...
Molly and then again, no.
Anja ... and no
Both (not quite in unison) Put it like
this. When you live with a writer, especially a
vulture like him, you're going to get picked
clean at some point

BEAT

Molly You're gonna get betrayed... and I'm not
talking with other women... I'm talking
betrayal on a deeper level than that; a betrayal
of your absolute self... your core....
Anja He'd steal your soul, if he could. Bastard!
And yeah... knowing he'd do that, hurts.

Soul theft: April 23rd 2013, *Fragments of Journeys Towards the Horizon* was read in Galway, Ireland. Amongst the audience were my friend's widow, his daughter, brother, best friend and the Dutch writer, van den Berg...

... you're not the only friend I have journeyed with, not the only friend! Who? Does it matter who? What do you want, a list? I don't care if you believe me! I don't fucking care! (BEAT) Ok, if you must know, his name was Fergus! Yes, 'was'. His name 'was' Fergus, and he drove a car... What else do you need to know about him? Did I walk with him? (BEAT) Did I walk with him... I walked away from him...

It had been only a year since the death of my Irish friend.[8] In my mind, and eager to suck blood, enough time had elapsed between the event

---

[8] Michael Diskin (*Fergus*) was the Director of The Town Hall Theatre, Galway. He also oversaw the re-building of the Lyric Theatre, Belfast. *Go raibh mille maith aghat*, my friend.

and its documentation. However, it became obvious, post reading, that a vampire's sense of time is relative. The loss was still raw in the minds of both family and close friends; time had yet to heal the mortal soul.

After the reading, there was silence. The close friends and family were not angry—rather they were in shock. It was not that I had betrayed his memory (the play is dedicated to my dear friend), it was that I had chronicled the truth (warts 'n all), rather than made a fiction/myth of the man and our experiences of him. In their minds, I had stolen not only the deceased's soul, but a part of their collective soul. There was a vampire in their midst where once there was a sympathetic soul.

There is a saying in Welsh (my native tongue): *"nes na'r hanesydd at y gwir, mae'r dramodydd sydd yn gelwydd oll i gyd."* ("The dramatist, who is full of fiction is closer to truth than the historian who is full of fact"—my trans.) Had I crossed into the historian's camp?

The events related above have caused me to question my modus operandi and the moral obligations of a creative vampire. Even though I place testimonies ("sucked souls") into broader dramatic contexts, thereby creating juxtaposing metaphors, acquaintances still confront their "raw truths" within my plays; which, by appropriation, become my truths. I suck souls, claim them as my own, then spew them out upon the stage barely digested; the sources still, at times, recognizable, at other times, mistakenly claimed (which is possibly worse).

The dilemma: Some could say that my vampire process betrays a lack of imagination? Obviously, I would dispute it; it is conscious stratagem. I exploit myself primarily, and secondarily, those that touch upon me. Surely writers/artists/vampires have always done this ("subject rape")? Am I any different? Is it just a matter of degrees of difference; degrees of honesty, truth, sucking? "And," as a colleague once assured me, "If we do not tell certain truths, they would not be told. What's more immoral? The telling or the silence?"

Is it therefore, possibly not an issue of content, rather one of form? Do people prefer to see the distorted mirror image as opposed to the true reflection? When true reflection is presented, is it rejected as it is not what is asked (or needed) of theatre? Does reality impinge upon the artifice? There again, perhaps it is a matter of format? Would a piece of literature—read in isolation—have been more palatable than the communal dramatic statement? Unfortunately, I have always envisaged my testimonies in dramatic form. I cannot betray my own vision... ah, betrayal! In *Fragments of Journeys Towards the Horizon*, I wrote...

Is that why you, we, somehow fail to create a context between us? You were compromised once, you don't want to be compromised again. (BEAT) You don't want to lose another friend through collaboration? Sure, I can understand that. Damn right.... Why didn't you tell me this earlier? I've been fucking pushing you.... I'm sorry. I just needed, I didn't... sorry. (BEAT) So how did this so called 'friend' betray you? (BEAT) He stole your dreams, after you'd trusted him with them. I see. Well I can tell you now, hand on heart, I'd never do that, I tread softly; dreams are fucking personal things, I'd never take those from you— borrow maybe, but I'd never steal them. Fuck, there's a bond of trust between us. Between friends. And in my book, the man who breaks that bond, deserves a fate worse than cancer. Your so called 'mate' deserves to be locked in a big black plastic box, and the insides should be completely covered in mirrors and shit, and he should be left alone for eternity to reflect upon his crime in a perpetual Droste effect of shame...Fuck him!

(N.B. Mark the deliberate self-deprecation (on Eliot's scale) and obfuscation around borrowing/stealing, thereby disguising my true and devious intent—to suck soul. Mark also, that Droste is a make of Dutch drinking chocolate. Upon its label is an image of a woman mirrored into infinity)

Perhaps, it would be better if I were to put an end to the deception; a self-staking to the heart of a reluctant yet voracious vampire—shades of Kane's autolysis? Unfortunately, I bear witness, and I am compelled to document—as the Greek proto-historian, Herodotus documented— the subjective and dramatic truth. For surely, it is only the sum of all subjective truths that go to make up the objective truth. *Ipso facto*, all truths are valid, even the truths of reluctant vampires. My plays are my truth. I cannot apologize for this? I dare not apologize.

And so, souls beware. I will continue to feed, and I feel a hunger upon me...

Ian Rowlands is a director/dramatist in TV, radio and theatre in his native Wales. At the time of publication, he is directing *Pobol y Cwm* (a Welsh language soap opera) for the BBC, continuing his collaboration with Jeroen van den Berg upon *Fragments of Journeys towards the Horizon* and finalizing a new play, *Water Wars* for National Theatre Wales.

FORNES AND ARTISTIC MENTORSHIP

Anne García-Romero

Artists need mentors to expand understanding of craft and methods of innovation in their field. Mentors can empower a younger generation by sharing approaches to hone and develop artistic voice. I studied playwriting with Maria Irene Fornes before and during graduate school. Her mentorship transformed my writing and my comprehension of the options available for those who create works for the theater. Fornes began teaching playwriting in 1966 at the Judson Workshop in New York City and continued to train generations of playwrights for approximately thirty-five years at universities, theaters and playwriting organizations across the U.S. as well as internationally including Mexico, India, Scotland and England. Fornes's pedagogy radically departs from more traditional schools of playwriting that focus on rising action, climax and resolution. Originally trained as a painter, Fornes utilizes many fine art techniques in her teaching, including visualization, portrait drawing and constructing set models. Fornes encourages the development of each playwright's individual voice over and above any cultural, political or aesthetic agenda. She privileges each playwright's unique process versus a prescribed formula.

Character creation is the cornerstone of Fornes's pedagogy. Rather than instructing her students to generate an airtight structure that focuses on conflict, Fornes guides playwrights through a process that helps them intuitively connect to character, which can then become the play's foundation. Fornes seems more interested in the genesis of an idiosyncratic character-driven theatrical world than a pre-determined well-made construction. She also encourages multiplicity of ideas, forms and cultural influences on the path toward writing a play.

The power of Fornes's presence and the generative access she provides has inspired me deeply. Her method catapults me right into the center of my creativity as a playwright, with the task of internally and subjectively discovering the play I need to write. This intuitive and artistically innovative methodology has largely influenced my path as a playwright and teacher. Though her formal teaching career ended in the mid-2000s due to her declining health, Fornes and her work continue to guide me.

Fornes, now 84, suffers from Alzheimer's disease. In 2013, Morgan Jenness, her agent, and Michelle Memran, a filmmaker who has spent the last decade creating *The Rest I Make Up*, a documentary about Fornes, valiantly galvanized the theater community to support an ailing Fornes and successfully advocated for her transfer from a residence in upstate New York to one in upper Manhattan where her students and colleagues could consistently spend time with her. I now live in the Midwest but have visited my beloved mentor during trips to Manhattan. I kept in mind the advice from friends that Maria Irene now responds most to music and Spanish. During my first visit, after I enter her room alone, I turn on her CD player and the joyful rhythms and forceful tone of Cuban singer, Albita, fill the air. Then, I begin to speak to her in Spanish: *"Maria Irene eres maravillosa, increible, te quiero mucho. Cuanto me alegro verte."* (Maria Irene, you are marvelous, incredible, I love you very much. I'm so happy to see you.)

As the Caribbean ballads continue, she whispers, *"Cuba."* Fornes left Cuba when she was 14 and these childhood memories now surface as she runs her fingers from her eyes down her cheeks to indicate tears. I gently touch her arms and begin to hold her hand. I recall that one of my playwriting colleagues who had visited did 'hand dancing' with her and so I slowly move her hands in mine while our arms sway to the music. As the third song plays, a notable shift occurs and she starts talking to me in non-stop Spanish. Sometimes her sentences are linear, other times they end with a repetition of words like *"Mamá"* or *"Papá."* I do my best to engage in conversation. She seems to tell me a story about what might have been a childhood friend who had something taken out of her hands. She at one point declares, *"Soy bonita, Maria Irene Fornes...very beautiful."* She later slowly caresses my arms and then my face. She says, *"Besito"* and beckons me forward so she can kiss my cheek. We continue 'hand dancing' while I smile, relishing the moment. Next, she orders, *"No. Más serio"* and I realize she is directing me to be more serious. She then begins to make grand gestures with her face and arms and I start to mirror her. She laughs and looks at me straight in the eye. She points to herself and then to me.

After I say goodbye, a veil descends and that vacant look once again

ANNE GARCÍA-ROMERO   **99** transforms her into an elderly woman with Alzheimer's. However, I leave her room feeling incredibly moved and infinitely grateful. In the classroom, Maria Irene Fornes taught me to explore language, form, character and structure in remarkable ways that empower my theatrical voice. In her residence room, she teaches me to use language, gesture, memory and music to profoundly engage one another. She continues to show me that always, the artistic spirit endures.

Anne García-Romero's book, *The Fornes Frame: Contemporary Latina Playwrights and the Legacy of Maria Irene Fornes*, is forthcoming from University of Arizona Press. Her plays include *Provenance, Paloma, Earthquake Chica, Mary Peabody in Cuba*, and *Santa Concepción*. Her plays are published by Broadway Play Publishing, Playscripts, Smith & Kraus and NoPassport Press. She's an Assistant Professor in the Department of Film, Television and Theatre at the University of Notre Dame and a Resident Playwright at Chicago Dramatists. *www.annegarciaromero.com*

ALIGNING A VISION

Caridad Svich

Making new work for live performance demands every bit of fiber and muscle, sinew and strength, heart and mind just to make happen. Sometimes as an artist you wish to speak to the now; sometimes you wish to speak with and to the dead; at other times, you wish to interact with history, and at others still, with the vast unknown: future time, and real, nonlinear time: time devoid of clocks and watches and markers—what I like to call "fluid time." Form and content go hand in hand. The container must complement and/or frame the art object. Another way to think of this: the form must seem somehow invisible, as if upon witnessing the object, the viewer need think "I can't imagine this piece any other way."

Often in the world of new writing for the stage, the talk tends to circle around "formal innovation." How is the piece for live performance "different from other plays?" "What is new about it?" Etc. Form for form's sake, however, does not innovation make. It need go hand in hand with content. Shiny new forms may be just that—attractive vector points on the page of Drama. When form and function are indivisible, then, only then does the work, in its distinctive unity rise.

We can point to artists that have changed and keep changing how we think about theatre and live performance through the ages. In Western drama and performance alone, names such as Euripides, Shakespeare, Bertolt Brecht, Federico Garcia Lorca, Tennessee Williams, Samuel Beckett, Edward Bond, Harold Pinter, Howard Barker, Ping Chong, Robert Lepage, Simon McBurney, Ariane Mnouchkine, Peter Stein, Robert Woodruff, Ivo van Hove, Luis Valdez, Pina Bausch, Adrienne Kennedy, Maria Irene Fornes, Sam Shepard, Richard Foreman, Bill Viola, Mac Wellman, Bernard-Marie Koltes, Stephen Sondheim, Sarah Kane, Tony Kushner, Suzan-Lori Parks, Milcha Sanchez-Scott, Rinde Eckert, Enda Walsh and many, many more. The list is wide-ranging. Think about the times when you feel as if you have felt awake in the theatre again—that feeling of wanting to put your hand on something, but not knowing quite how, how to even apprehend its occurrence, only the knowledge that it has occurred.

The first time that Samuel Beckett's *Waiting for Godot* (1953) was experienced must have been one of these times. The first time I saw Tim Crouch's *My Arm* (2003) was definitely one of these times. It's all about the moment. The moment of contact. It differs for each of us in the field, time and again, and also, depending on where we are in our own artistic journey/path. Consider, in the world of fiction, for example, encountering Virginia Woolf's writing for the first time, or the work of Octavia Butler, Jeannette Winterson, Colson Whitehead, Ali Smith, Michael Joyce, Junot Diaz, Gabriel Garcia Marquez or Chris Ware, to name only a few of the many, many who have changed the way we think, feel, and see the world.

The awareness of new-ness is there. Sometimes quite blatantly in the markings on the page, in the manner, in effect, in which the page is marked, and sometimes in ways much more subterranean and apparent over time. Visionary work doesn't occur in an instant. Sometimes it doesn't even know it is visionary at all. Sometimes it just is: the expression of a moment, this moment, and the form, with craft and discipline and practice, finds itself at one with the content. Innovation, in other words, is not necessarily found by seeking out what's new in the toolbox, or even if it is labelled or categorized by someone else as being new. Innovation is part of an artist's journey—if they are lucky enough to strive for excellence and keep their ear to the ground. Street-wear in one city becomes fashion in another in a year or two's time, to use one analogy.

The ground upon which you walk in the daily practice of the craft and re-visioning it—chasing the impulses that say "gotta make this now," as opposed to "the market says I gotta make this"—is a slippery, often precarious and perilous ground of doubt and fear.

Envisioning requires something of an imbalance, born out of resistance and challenge. Unlike, say, designing a car—however beautiful—innovation in the arts is not a utilitarian enterprise. The mark of innovation may not announce itself through sure test drive and an immaculate design; the mark may be rough and strange and misshapen at first and only over and through time find its proper alignment, and when it does so, then turn, and find another mark unknown that will pave yet another way. Innovation is not a static thing. And it cannot be quantified. No one can write like Beckett. Look at how many have failed trying to enter and imitate his theatre of beautiful failure and despair. Innovation, if the artist is alert to her/his/trans daily practice and willing to embrace the fumbles and stumbles and going sometimes wide or near the mark, yields. Think, for example, of when Caryl Churchill moved into writing for and exploring dance-theatre, and how as a result something as rare and unexpected and truly art-changing occurred such as *The Skriker* (1994). Consider Martin Crimp's *Attempts on Her Life* (1997)—a play unlike any other that still, today, challenges and defies everything we think about when we think about new writing in English, at least.

How, then, to chart innovation and moreover, to support it? I don't think there are any quantifiable graphs that can be made. How can there be if one is defying, with the art and its process, what is quantifiable to begin with? But I do think that time and space for dreaming and re-visioning are crucial. In effect, the job in the theatre industry, I think, on the administrative end, is to ask the artists what they need, and not to design a program geared toward innovation, because, unlike cars, to use that analogy again, art isn't a numbers job. It's soul work. It's culture work, and it takes a whole lotta faith and big leaps just to make it happen at all, let alone grant it the space to happen.

Now, here's the thing, and it is the tricky thing about theatre: it is a collaborative medium. So, unlike, say, hiding away writing the novel or the poem, it demands the testing of ideas and forms and signs in space in time. You see, an artist's path is a path. It is not a series of results, and innovation, therefore, is not apparent. It's trial and error and sometimes a whole lotta both before the lightning strikes, that is, if the pursuit and/or the stay on the path is constant. It's much easier to give up and/or stay in the known groove than to venture outside into the wilderness of the field—and here I mean the field of art itself— intangible and metaphorical—and knock about and bloody well hope something will, with will and determination and skill and craft and talent, hold water. And even then, nobody may see it. You see, that is the other thing about innovation: sometimes you don't see it right away. Sometimes it sneaks up on you. Sometimes it takes several viewings— in fact, I would argue that it does take several viewings—and listenings and soundings—to be witness-ed/seen/felt.

So, in this journey focused on artistic innovation, how do we begin to really query the field as a whole? Without focusing on, say, text-message and Twitter plays (although they're cool and all that) as a way to talk about innovation? We all know that the work, the true work of query, goes beyond one of a singular, actionable encounter. Might we ask ourselves instead how a path is made? How is a path nurtured and fostered and tended?

In times of little means, an old Spanish saying goes, we will still have plenty. One of the constant refrains that circles among and within the subtext of so many conversations about theatre-making is one of, well, money itself:

Ask most artists what they want, and by and large, time and money will be at the top of the list.

Time to make work without thinking about money. Money to make work to buy time.

Think of the gestation periods of most plays and the fragile economies and ecologies of an industry that perforce, if it believes in its artists and their personal visions, must find a way to support the making of a work of art. Now, the industry itself doesn't have, let's say, an obligation to its artists—or wait, doesn't it? This debate also circles amongst practitioners late nights in pubs and living rooms over wine and other things.

Are we all now dependent on crowd-funding?

Must every play come with a kickstarter campaign to make it happen?

How many hours will that take? And when does the art get made?

How does one budget one's time and money and no money to actually move forward in the beautiful game we call innovation or better said: the pursuit of seeing the world anew?

I am an optimist. Better said: I am a creative optimist.

I believe in the power of art. I use the word "art" without shame.

I use the word "poetry" too without shame, for I believe theatre—the event of it, the making of it—at its best, is poetry in motion.

I also believe in the right to fail.

Without it, as art-makers, we are nothing.

Without it, as producers and presenters, we are nothing.

Without it, audiences will never know the beauty of what radical innovation holds: namely, revolution, invention and transfiguration in culture, art, society and love.

ACT THREE

TASK

INNOVATION IN WRITING

Octavio Solis

When I think of innovation in the theatre, I can't help but summon up writing examples, which is understandable, since I am first and foremost a playwright myself. I'm always struggling to keep my writing fresh by treading on new ground, and the inspiration I draw from my colleagues is not to be underestimated. I have had many startling moments in the theatre when a particular writer executed something dramatically new and untried in his or her work. An experiment with language. A devising of new structural forms for storytelling. A rethinking of particular characters or tropes. An unconscious exorcism of the rules we follow when we write for the stage. But the one consistent thread that all my brushes with innovation have in common is the writers' insistent and persuasive way of seeing. It begins inevitably with their singular vision.

My first experience with the kind of contemporary innovation came when I saw *The Woman: Scenes of War and Freedom* by Edward Bond at London's National Theatre. Here this celebrated playwright took the familiar war myths of the Greeks and stretched them beyond what seemed dialectically possible in order to shed new light on our contemporary obsession with war. The fiery intellect of Bond shaped even the acting styles. I'd never seen anything like that before. But I quickly understood something about history. I learned that it's not a rigid palette upon which human events are indelibly etched, but that the past is a living organism subject to the actions of the present. We change the past every time we look at it, and in the theatre, we inhabit it to serve our needs.

Harold Pinter has long been an accomplished and admired writer, and most of us have been familiar with his works. There's an approach to the world that brands his works with that unique Pinteresque touch. It's a world where the unknown is just out of view, a world where people act out of a palpable sense of menace and madness. On that score alone, he is an innovator. But what he did with his masterpiece *Betrayal* completely upended our understanding of narrative structure. He reversed time and arranged his scenes (with some exceptions) from the last moment to the first. We began to perceive human impulses and gestures differently as we turned inevitability and fate on its head. Our concerns were not with how things would end up but rather how they would begin, for there the seed of crime was sown.

Suzan-Lori Parks is a writer I have been lucky to have known in my lifetime. I consider her one of our great geniuses. Each of her plays is a radical gem of striking language and syncopation. The molecules in her world operate in much the same way they do in Samuel Beckett's darkest works. But as I saw in *The America Play*, Suzan-Lori's molecules vibrate to the rhythm of Modern Jazz. In this work, we contemplate a new vision of Lincoln and his assassination and its place in post-modern African-American life. Plot and traditional narrative are dispensed with in favor of the sequence of gestures and repetitive text dynamics. Her play enters our consciousness not through the front door but through the back, where it sidesteps our received notions of history and politics and art. And still, the work crescendos toward a catharsis that catches us off guard, for in the end, her work is as rigorously emotional as it is intellectual.

I had another more recent encounter with the audacious genius of Taylor Mac, when his epic *The Lily's Revenge* took the Magic Theatre by storm. The world according to Mac, represented over five remarkable acts, exhibited a kind of engorged Blakean spirituality. The spoken text in the work, both florid and profane, soared to such complex and ecstatic heights that it reinvented language. And its devotion to the body restored to us the joys of sweet carnality that AIDS had robbed us of back in the 80's. Watching this work, I felt like much of the world must have felt when they first encountered the iconoclastic Romantic poets of the early 19th Century.

All four of these writers have an irrepressible and uncompromising vision of the world that runs counter to how we normally experience it. Executing that vision comes at a cost. It means dispensing with the familiar at the risk of alienating the audience. It means grinding against how things are usually done and butting against those opposed to "thinking different." It often means the work doesn't often get produced, at least not immediately, for these works have an unmistakable surge about them. But for these writers and many others I have known and revered, there is no other option. It's not about a conceit that one puts on for the sake of novelty like a new suit of clothes. It's not done to be cute or opaque or fashionable. It is simply how they see. The processes of time and space, the modes of communication, the physics of the landscape they create are all subject to how they process the world. Theirs is a skewed, sometimes painful and often mysterious lens we look through, but given a chance, that lens can reveal something wholly unique and truthful about each of us. And that's a straight-up lesson for the rest of us writers and artists.

Arthur Rimbaud's biographer Jean-Luc Steinmetz said of his *Illuminations*, "Rimbaud hallucinates and creates an epic." In a sense, that's what our most innovative writers do. The world is their hallucination, and it is up to us to make it ours.

We created it.... Let's take it over.
(Patti Smith at the conclusion of "My Generation")

Octavio Solis is a playwright and director currently based in Ashland, Oregon and formerly based in San Francisco. His award-winning plays include *Lydia, Dreamlandia, Santos & Santos,* and *Se Llama Cristina.* He is published by Broadway Play Publishing, NoPassport Press, and Playscripts.

WRITE IT YOURSELF!

Oliver Mayer

"No mames, guey!"
"No jodas, tu!"
"No seas tan boludo!"

Take your pick. All three phrases say roughly the same thing, yet all three carry an unmistakable particularity that only begins with their regional identity. All three are what one might term street Spanish— but these are three very different streets, separated by continents and time zones and nationalities, much less lived history. When writing dialogue, the colloquial distinctions between Mexican, Caribbean and Argentine realities literally hang in the balance of one's literary choice. One might think that a smart writer—or at least one who had done a little research—would choose wisely from the three phrases and pick the one that fit the streets of the story being told. But one would be largely wrong—at least in the world of current teleplays and screenplays being shot on both U.S. coasts. Instead of choosing one of the three, or even better inventing a new and better phrase to capture the reality and identity of the street in question, the preponderance of contemporary movies and television script writers don't even try to write in Spanish (or for that matter any other foreign language) when their stories take them onto streets where English isn't the only language. Rather, the accepted current choice is to simply write the English equivalent— "Don't fuck with me!" or "Don't be such a jerk!"—and then to wait for the auditioning actor to translate it for them.

This places the bilingual actor in question in a strange position, to say the least. More often than not, the audition material is longer and more substantial than the above example. Just as often, the casting director, producers, writer and director don't know enough Spanish to tell the difference between Mexican, Cuban or Argentine vernaculars. And sometimes the auditioning actor has a tenuous grip on the Spanish language too, having forgotten or never having learnt idiomatic phrases like the above ones in the first place. Yet the translation must be made. The scene will be shot one way or the other and then shown on some kind of screen to the world. A writer will get credit for having written not simply the scene but those newly translated words, and may even receive an award from his or her peers for the work in question. Meanwhile, the chosen actor shoots the scene and moves on to the next role, the next audition—and the next translation on the fly.

What to do?

Before we try to answer, let's add a bit more to this growing conundrum. Often, in an audition room where the writer, casting director, producers and director do not know the difference between *"No jodas tu!"* or *"No seas tan boludo!"* they hire someone whom they believe does indeed have such knowledge and mastery. This person—termed an expert—becomes very powerful very quickly. The trouble is that this expert is often not an experienced professional and has not gone through anywhere near the process of auditioning or rewriting that actors and writers must endure along the way to success in their chosen fields. Often these experts know one thing well—perhaps an element within the storyline—but are just as tenuous with idiomatic Spanish as everyone else in the room, although they will never admit it. Yet because of the vacuum created by need and lack of knowledge, the expert becomes the arbiter. Invariably, mistakes and even illegalities occur; actors are asked where they are from, trespassing clear actors' union rules much less federal regulations regarding discrimination. Actors who admit to, say, Caribbean backgrounds are then denied the chance to advance on projects centered in Mexico or Argentina. Other actors are forced to lie about their parentage in order to get the role. Still others may be lucky enough to have the right nationality for said expert and may get the role—and then prove to be ill-suited to the actual role, or in other words, bad actors. No wonder that so many television shows and films are cringe-worthy when it comes to Latino/a presentations, storylines and dialogue.

Is there a way to fix something this badly broken?

There is certainly no easy fix in sight, other than the slow but steady infiltration of the Industry by Latinos. Case in point: Cuban-born show runner Cynthia Cidre has brought new life into the DALLAS franchise not simply by re-imagining the Ewing family 20-some years later with the next generation of attractive Stetson-wearing philandering snakes in the grass but by including Latinos in the storyline, some wearing white hats and some wearing distinctly black ones. The cliffhanger of the second season involves the revelation that the Ewings stole their very ranch land from the Ramos clan around the time of the Texas annexation in the 19th Century, and that now mother Carmen and daughter Elena have the ancient deeds in their hands. Whether this means that Carmen can stop being the Ewing cook and housekeeper and can start to dress like Linda Grey and redecorate South Fork in Southwestern styles remains to be seen; but this development would never have happened without a true expert at the helm. And by expertise I mean not only that Cidre is fully bilingual and bicultural, but that she is also a fully vetted professional, the creator of the much-loved CANE, and highly respected throughout the Industry.

Similarly, a growing pool of fine actors are gaining hard experience traversing the Scylla and Charybdis of auditions and text translations, finding their way onto the screen and making the material literally better than it deserves to be. This is not a solution by any means; in some ways it only exacerbates the problem. Now writers feel more empowered to let actors do their research for them, particularly when no one calls them out for their laziness and inexactitude. Still, it is not quite so cringe-inspiring to see seasoned pros at work, demonstrating their acting abilities in two languages, and making the very best of an awful situation.

Do they deserve some kind of writing credit? Damned right they do. Will it ever happen?

Perhaps the answer is up to all of us.

Oliver Mayer is the author of nearly 30 plays, from *Blade to the Heat* to his most recent, *The Sinner From Toledo,* inspired by a Chekhov short story. He also writes opera libretti and children's books, and teaches at the University of Southern California's School of Dramatic Arts.

ON ECO-THEATER

Jeremy Pickard

Eight years ago I made a play about waste, assuming it would be a singular jaunt in environmental themes. Now I collaborate with climate scientists, run an eco-playwriting program for Brooklyn 5th-graders, and am beginning work on the eighth in a series of ecology-inspired Planet Plays. I am searching for a new mode of theater, not because there is a need to reinvent the wheel, but because I believe that a holistic approach—tethering content, process, and production to complex environmental questions—is my best chance at making good art and a difference in the world.

To paraphrase Anne Bogart, theater proposes a model of how we might live in the world; every production is a microcosm of society at large, an arena where a community of individuals gathers each day and attempts to make something together. What we make and how we make it depends on what is invested and what is valued.

I choose to value ecology because I want my art to ignite conversations about our relationship to the environment. I choose to value sustainability because it is the future, and because every definition of the word implies endurance, discipline, and creativity. Inspired by the resourcefulness of children and the definition of eco which means "house", I call my theater company a Clubhouse, because I want my organization to remain grassroots, non-profit, community-driven, and playful. I continue to fill this symbolic Clubhouse with a gaggle of artists and environmental experts who work on a project-to-project basis. I call them Superheroes, as I do anyone who is using his or her creativity to better the Earth. Together we make eco-plays, practice green production, gather as a community, and talk about the world.

To be sure, it's all an experiment. There is no real precedent for eco-theater as a modality. Performance artists have long made work inspired by the natural world, but not necessarily eco-theater in the way I am attempting to define it. And if our culture has any expectations about eco-theater, they are not necessarily the kind that excite and inspire. The term often seems to evoke an evening filled with dense and didactic discussions, a revival of old-school political drama. Personally I have more interest in dance than I do old-school political drama; still, the misconception of eco-theater as tedious and self-righteous is one of many obstacles that I have yet to fully overcome. I am a scientist in the field, asking questions, continuously trying and failing.

Writing about eco-theater, I am struck with a conundrum. I do not wish to preach, for who am I to tell fellow artists what the content of their plays should be, or that it is their duty to recycle building materials? Other than encourage, all I can do is my work. But I also want to be as effective as possible, and artists who actively practice sustainability, let alone holistic eco-theater, are the extreme minority. It occurs to me that if I actually care about making an impact, I can't be the only one doing it.

Tangible, Green Theater

Australian artist Tanja Beer is an eco-designer, in both philosophy and practice. She has constructed expansive sets that can fit into a single backpack, created worlds out of ready-made backstage equipment, transformed old plastic into acrobatic silks, and dressed a stage with hundreds of local apples (which she then donated to children's charities). Currently completing her PhD, Tanja is focused on tackling one of eco-theater's great obstacles—the theater space itself—by designing and constructing living stages. Built from things like donated vegetable crates and inspired by the agriculture of the area, her living stages are part actors' playground and part community garden; indeed, engaging with the community is a major goal. Locals help Tanja grow and tend the plants that become the stage, set, props, and refreshments. Audiences are welcome to nibble on the scenery before the show starts, after which the space becomes an interactive theater where performers climb, tell stories, and eat. After the production closes, the greenery is replanted in the community.

In reference to how we make artistic decisions in directing and design, we often say that the needs of the script trump all. This is an important rule, and honoring the playwright and maintaining a consistent vision are values many of us share. But if we also value sustainability, and the needs of the script demand that we make artistic decisions that negatively affect the way we live in the world, which value is trumped? In other words: what is our global responsibility as people who use nonrenewable resources to make temporary experiences? If an author values the preservation of trees but her publisher cannot use recycled paper, how does she publish the book?

The ethical dilemmas are as difficult as the environmental ones, and I'm not about to solve them. We are free artists; there is no law preventing us from using foam core and luan, curtailing the amount of water and chemicals we use laundering costumes, or capping our electricity use while we tech long shows with old lights. But there are also few incentives (economic or otherwise) supporting more efficient approaches; it is still cheaper and easier to throw an entire Broadway set into one dumpster than it is to hire multiple crews to sort, recycle, and store what is salvageable.

Assuming these incentives are slow in coming, we can problem-solve in other ways. I'll take a good guess and suppose that most shows are designed with the dumpster as a given. To green a production without an added economic burden requires considering sustainability much earlier in the process. To quote Tanja's website: "Just as an experienced stage designer generally designs with budget limitations in mind, I also incorporate an environmentally responsible approach to the way in which I create work. This begins early in the design process, and is integrated into every aspect of the procedure—from the development of conceptual ideas, to the realization of the design concept, to the manner in which the finished product is disposed of."

This kind of "cradle to cradle" planning requires intense cooperation between the artistic team, the producers, and the owners of the performance space itself. But even if complete collaboration is not currently attainable, a designer with a commitment to sustainability can still make waves on her own. NYC's best example of this is Donyale Werle, a powerhouse designer and a vocal advocate for sustainable practices. She works across the spectrum of commercial to independent theater, and all of her sets and props are handcrafted out of salvaged materials regardless of whether or not she was hired to "be green". Audiences attending her Tony-winning production of *Peter and the Starcatcher* might not have known that the grand proscenium was constructed out of discarded kitchenware, or that upstage panels of glass were actually doors recovered from an East Village bodega fire, or that her studio in Brooklyn (Paper Mâché Monkey) produces just an inch of trash each day. Donyale maintains that she can build scenery out of anything, and has called what she does "storytelling with bits and pieces of our existing lives."

It's not up to the rest of us to wait for high-profile leaders to create a precedent. Getting to know Tanja and Donyale, I've come to understand that their designs are not particularly complicated or expensive, nor do they lack artistic merit or require artistic sacrifice; on the contrary, they are often cheap, easy, and effective, offering new possibilities in the rehearsal room and unique visual storytelling to audiences. What Tanja and Donyale offer by example are practical approaches to design that could be used and reinterpreted by anyone, from carpenters volunteering at their local community theater to resident designers at repertory houses.

Imagine a regional or off-Broadway theater devoting an entire season to green production. Think of how many ingenious designers and managers would meet the call-to-arms with immense creativity and pride—something the theater could brag about, audiences could wonder at, and the press could promote as game-changing. Imagine the college drama programs that would follow suit and how many future professionals would grow up knowing creative green solutions not as cute anomalies or fashionable trends, but as increasingly standardized ways of making theater.

When Superhero Clubhouse begins a new project, we start designing by determining what we have and what we need before dreaming about what we want. Our budgets are often small, and it is important to me that I pay my collaborators, so money for design materials is usually minimal. This is not taken as a snub by the designers I work with, but as a challenge. R.B. Schlather describes designing with my company as a process of "creating maximal images through minimal means." By understanding and embracing our sustainable values, R.B. allowed us to go to *MARS (a play about mining)* with nothing onstage but a bucket, and to travel between the dual worlds of farm and city in *SATURN (a play about food)* simply with a carefully curated selection of used chairs. In both productions, the choice to work with minimalism kept things green, but it also put more attention on the bodies and voices of our multi-talented performers whose athleticism and physical storytelling prowess were qualities we wanted to feature.

Minimalism is an aesthetic choice that I like to work with, but it is not a formula for making green theater. Michael Minahan and Preesa Adeline Bullington build epic and magical worlds for our annual Big Green Theater Festival, scavenging sidewalks, thrift stores, and Craig's List as well as local re-use centers like Materials for the Arts and Build It Green. Together with Jay Maury, whose ambitious lighting designs are made entirely of LED, fluorescent, and household instruments, our designers transform The Bushwick Starr Theater every April into an immersive green playground. The choice to "go big" feels necessary—it both honors the untamed stories of our ten-year-old playwrights and charms the local Bushwick audiences, allowing for our community to engage in the environmental themes of the plays with surprise and delight.

Connecting Everything

Undoubtedly, theater artists can be leaders in the global environmental movement. By visibly valuing sustainability in our production practices, we ally with environmentalists and proclaim that our relationship to the natural world is something worth talking about.

But to me, green theater production is only one part of eco-theater. I am interested in how all aspects of theater-making might connect to my environmental values. In an eco-system, it is impossible to isolate one species without considering the many other species and natural forces that act upon it. So I want to consider and connect everything in my theatrical ecosystem, from script to strike.

As Anne Washburn shows us so magnificently in *Mr. Burns, A Post-Electric Play*, theater is how we began, and it is what we return to in face of great adversity. In *Mr. Burns*, when a catastrophe permanently shuts off the electricity and thrusts the world into chaos, survivors use the basic tools of theater to begin building a new society out of the stories that remain. We may not face an electric apocalypse in reality, but the stakes of our actual global environmental problems are just as high.

I believe eco-theater is ultimately about defining and articulating new mythologies for a tumultuous and changing world. As the planet warms, as extreme weather throws what we love into precarious positions, and as basic necessities and securities become increasingly more threatened, the status quo upon which we've been making plays for so long will shift, and so must our stories.

Already, our changing environment is changing us. Here in New York City, we're mounting productions in the midst of record hot summers and unpredictable winters that increase our use of inefficient air conditioning and heat. We're dashing to rehearsals drinking imported coffee in disposable Styrofoam cups, eating take-out made from factory-farmed meat and genetically modified corn products, and navigating a subway system still recovering from the effects of Superstorm Sandy. We're writing plays on laptops powered by coal from ancient American mountain ranges now permanently destroyed, and printing one-sided scripts on paper made from endangered old-growth forests. Ecology is the silent conflict at the heart of our days. Can't it also be at the heart of our plays?

At least, this is the question I am asking myself. Not all artists feel agenda-driven, but I do. I feel responsible to use my art form—an art form particularly good at stimulating change of thought—to address the most pressing issues humanity currently faces. The environmental science community is eager for artists to be the harbingers of a cultural revolution in which the tree-hugging minority evolves into a policy-shifting majority. Theater artists have the influence of intimacy and the power of imagination. We may not be able to change government directly, but we can change minds, person to person and community to community, simply because we are engaged in the most primitive and intuitive human meme.

When the entire Planet Play series is complete, the nine plays will connect to each other in theme, character, and chronology, like an ecosystem and a mythological family tree. But the series will never really be "complete" any more than an ecosystem is absolute or a tree is static. This idea poses a problem for publishing, but at the moment I am more interested in the experiment of duration and change. When I began the series in 2005 I was 22 years old, and *An Inconvenient Truth* had not yet been released. Now, ten years later, articles relating to climate change appear nearly every day in the *New York Times*. Just as I am a different person, our cultural understanding and acceptance of environmental crises has matured immensely, and so my plays must change. In another ten years, they may need to change again.

How far might I go with connecting the play-making process to my environmental values? Can I make collaborating with scientists a priority? Can I create shorter plays for shorter techs and performances, thereby significantly decreasing my utility usage? Can I plan a tour strictly based on what will cause the smallest carbon footprint? Can I instigate a materials-sharing program with like-minded companies? Can I recycle my words, stories, and choreography over and over again? Can I splatter disclaimers on my grant applications, demanding green design and efficient production houses? Can I back up these demands by demanding more from myself? Once I ask the questions, once I decide that my values will directly influence not only what I make but also how I make it, the possibilities pour forth.

Impossible Questions

Environmental issues are complex. Recycling is important, but it does not stop the carbon-spewing cargo ships from carrying those bottles and cans to China and back, or the energy-intensive recycling plant that processes them. We may abhor fossil fuels, but it is currently not economically, technologically, or politically possible to convert to renewables in one fell swoop. We may value local food, but a world of small farms is unlikely to feed all 7.4 billion of us (let alone the anticipated 9-10 billion several decades from now).

Soon into the process of devising a new eco-play, my collaborators and I attempt to articulate an impossible question—one that cannot easily be answered, even by an expert. This "impossibility" allows for the play to grapple with the complexities of an environmental issue without coming to any conclusion, so that the question continues on in the minds of our audience long after the play has finished.

In *EARTH (a play about people)* our impossible question, "Should we have children?", makes for good eco-theater because it is both global and personal—global because the topic of overpopulation encompasses health, human rights, economic equality, food, water, immigration, and climate; personal because individuals are still drawn to have babies despite how aware we are of our progeny's inevitable environmental impact (or the impact of a volatile environment on our progeny). "Should we have children?" is a question few of us feel comfortable asking ourselves, let alone our friends and family; therefore, it is risky and exciting to explore onstage.

The impossible question can directly influence the play-making process. Researching *EARTH*, we came to understand overpopulation as a problem of limitation and communication across distance. So we imposed limitations on ourselves, and experimented with communicating across distance: the process became a unique collaboration between a group of NYC-based artists and scientists and several groups working remotely in cities like Bucharest and Guangzhou. Each remote group, working only with the resources they had available to them, created a five-minute scene based on a series of rules and prompts, and responding to the impossible question. The scenes—assembled together by a scripted framing device—were directed by several different directors. This way, we could see how "too many cooks in the kitchen" might find cohesion in the face of a problem that affects us all.

Limitation is essential at Superhero Clubhouse. Using the impossible question as an anchor, we apply temporal, physical and/or storytelling limitations to every project. In *Flying Ace and the Storm of the Century*, a play exploring preparation, adaptation, and innovation, we decided that our dog protagonist (inspired by Snoopy) would remain on top of a small doghouse for the entirety of the performance with nothing but a typewriter, a bottle, and his imagination for company. This wasn't just a stunt; we wanted to strand our dog in the middle of the ocean in order to ask hard questions about the situation many coastal communities face in relation to extreme climatic events like Superstorm Sandy.

The question for *URANUS (a play about waste)*, "What happens to our stuff?" allowed us to explore both the journey of trash and the unknown, daunting future of our disposable culture. In the second-draft production, our actors were limited to a small bank of physical gestures and a strict staging pattern; half way through the play, the action was rewound even as the text continued. This limitation of staging was a wonderful challenge for our actors, and it made our themes of cycles and entropy very visible.

Of course, limitations sometimes present themselves without being imposed; in this case, it's a question of how to embrace them. For *MERCURY (a play about poison)*, our first production in NYC, our poverty caused us to rehearse in a very small room. Instead of feeling forced to cope with the room until we were able to stretch our legs in a larger space, we took advantage of the limitations it provided, allowing the space to influence our story and staging. Based on the history of the Danbury, Connecticut hatting industry (the cause of rampant mercury poisoning in western CT as well as in the brains of many hat makers), we set the play in a cramped, one-room hat shop typical of 1780's New England, and allowed the restrictions of size to complement the mad mental journey our protagonist was to take.

I no longer feel inhibited by limitation, but liberated by it. This is in part due to collaborating with scientists, who thrive within constraints and recognize the importance of control in managing variables. As artists, we understand that great invention often comes from great limitation, yet we spend an immense amount of time seeking ideal resources and fighting against scarcity. Ecologically, we lost this fight long ago: we now know there is a limit to things like trees, clean air and fresh water. Today, environmentalists fight to protect the things we still have and to find creative ways of using them. Addressing the mega-droughts predicted for the western USA will require great creativity on the part of leaders and scientists regarding how water is distributed, how cities and agricultural systems rebuild themselves to accommodate drought, and how people in the future will live their daily lives. Similarly, the tenets of conservationism can inspire an eco-theater artist to shift focus away from loss and look instead at how best to innovate.

The Day that is to Come

I do not wish to be an activist, but an instigator; I do not wish to answer questions and demand change, but rather to ask questions and ignite thought. I want eco-theater to be a gathering place where people can wrestle environment questions with inspiration and even with joy, not batten down the hatches as they do battle with latent feelings of guilt and shame. For these reasons, the third essential component of my process is the search for and celebration of hope. We are lost as eco-theater artists if we spend a 90-minute performance lamenting the tragedies of our devastated environment. If our play is demanding that audiences "wake up!" we are not stimulating positive change but burdening our community with the same weariness they feel when skimming the headlines. Rather than a jarring alarm clock, why can't our wake-up call be an opening of curtains, a rooster's crow, the tickling of feet, or any number of other creative solutions that allow people to feel energized and hopeful about the day that is to come?

Many would say that we are past the point of no return, which means there is no choice but to raise the alarm. But culture changes slowly even as the Arctic melts swiftly. To properly address the state of our natural world, we must transform our global economic and cultural infrastructure (aka capitalism and consumerism) as we know it. This level of change requires cooperation, not just in governments and corporations, but also in our apartments and restaurants and theaters, and it will not happen overnight. If I am to be effective as an eco-theater artist, I must find a way to dance on the sweet spot between action and patience so that people can empower themselves to think differently, thereby slowly shifting the culture and communities around them. By using the ingenuity and creativity of theater to ponder impossible ecological questions, we are helping to nurture generations of independent thinkers, and hopefully create a better world.

Time will tell how eco-theater will fit into the fold. It rightfully hovers between the science community, interested primarily in education and outreach, and the theater world, interested primarily in good art. There are certainly kinks to work out, but I'm confident they will be, especially considering the trailblazing being done by set designers like Tanja Beer and Donyale Werle, lighting designers like James Bedell, playwrights like Chantal Bilodeau and Caridad Svich, choreographers like Jennifer Monson, green performance spaces like Wild Project and Center for Performance Research, and organizations like the Broadway Green Alliance, Center for Sustainable Practice in the Arts, and PositiveFeedback. I hope their work signals a movement; I'm excited to see what a new breed of resourceful and enterprising eco-artists will come up with. In the meantime, I'll keep experimenting.

Jeremy Pickard is the founder and captain of Superhero Clubhouse, a collective of artists and scientists working at the intersection of environmentalism and theater, for which he has been at the helm of over a dozen productions. Jeremy is a 2015 Artist-in-Residence with The Drama League and the Robert Rauschenberg Foundation.

ARTISTRY AND INNOVATION

Heather Woodbury

We may need a moratorium in the arts on the following words and phrases: In grant writing and program notes, the phrase "seeks to investigate...."; the word "community" (as applied to everything from a gang-ridden neighborhood to an aggregate of big business interests); the word "explore" where "look into" would do just fine; And yes, the word "innovation."

The usage of innovation is starting to piss me off. Most often these days, innovation is a byword for unexamined market-driven expansion. Innovate! Be innovative. Please explain to us, in 33 characters or less, how your idea is innovative!

Why are we innovating precisely and for whom? What do we mean when we say it and what's good for humanity and other living organisms about it? Why do we do it? Why should we? What does the role of the artist ask us to do with innovation? In particular how do we fulfill the role of the theatre artist as storyteller, and the role of theatre itself as living conduit for inchoate ritual? Innovation is more than an improvement or an invention. It is a renewal of purpose, a change; in art's case: a transformative change that intuits, perhaps precipitates, and certainly shapes—a paradigmatic shift.

Here's how innovation is touted in business and economic terms, in Wikipedia (uh, itself, I guess, an innovation on the encyclopedia):

"In society, innovation aids in comfort, convenience, and efficiency in everyday life. For instance, the benchmarks in railroad equipment and infrastructure added to greater safety, maintenance, speed, and weight capacity for passenger services. These innovations included wood to steel cars, iron to steel rails...diesel-powered to electric-diesel locomotives. By the mid-20th century, trains were making longer, faster...trips at lower costs for passengers. Other areas that add to everyday quality of life include the adoption of modems to cellular phones, paving the way to smart phones which supply the public with internet access any time or place.

'Innovation is the development of new customers value through solutions that meet new needs, or adding value to old customers by providing new ways of *maximizing* their current level of *productivity*. It is the *catalyst to growth*."

I'm not arguing that there is something inherently pernicious about all this fabulous growth. However, I do question the notion that growth is uniformly desirable, not to mention sustainable. As Jared Diamond notes in *Collapse*, for almost every technological innovation in human history, there is a corresponding unforeseen consequence, often one worse than the problem the innovation sought to address. (If this reminds you of a bad experimental play, it should!)

In his book *What Technology Wants*, Kevin Kelly defines all art, social institutions, and intellectual creations, all culture as part of a "self-reinforcing system of creation." He uses the term *technium* to identify all of this as tools human beings evolve to interpret and transform our reality. He then goes on to explain that this technium has a life of its own. That, much as we evolved from chimps, but are no longer chimps, the technium evolves from us but has its own biological intent.

Inventor, author and MIT wizard Ray Kurzweil has charted this biological momentum mathematically. He notes that one can't predict all the factors of how an organism will grow—the conditions are chaotic and random—however, one can predict with precision the rate of growth and the shape of that growth. That is almost always the same. Our mechanistic and systemic technology, he has correctly predicted so far, is growing at an unprecedented, exponential rate.

By around 2045, he says "the pace of change will be so astonishingly quick that we won't be able to keep up, unless we enhance our own intelligence by merging with the intelligent machines we are creating."

In theatre now, what's innovation? Is it to introduce new media? What about reducing media? In a culture of cyber-Faces, simulated sensory effects, corporate architecture that increasingly dominates collective space and the maximum availability of consumer-friendly brain candy, what constitutes true innovation? What about the media of masks, mimicry, minimal spectacle and maximal imagination? Is more aesthetic, technical, or even formal innovation what is needed to give us a spiritually audible experience of the reality we inhabit?

What can transform rather than transfix? Is it innovation of form, content or of purpose that is required of theatre now, at this present juncture in the human story?

I say we need to be careful lest we innovate mainly through gadgetry and ever-plateauing platforms: careful that we don't race artistically to keep up with the million-fold exponential growth, the inconceivable pace of technological evolution, while the human psyche advances by increments in slow and ancient cycles.

At the close of his turn-of-the-century masterpiece, the *U.S.A.* trilogy, John Dos Passos gives us the image of a young man walking along a highway in the Midwest. A car passes, and above him flies a new jet airplane, casting a huge shadow over the landscape, its speed dwarfing the boy's pace.

Perhaps the transformative power of theatre dwells in that vast chasm of time and space between the boy on the land—earth and us—and the plane in the sky—our ideas manifest. Is it possible that the intelligent machine we need to build is a stage sacred enough to contain our primitive souls?

For my part, I've responded to the current received wisdom of the dwindling attention span by making a twelve-hour serial about surviving in today's America on a planet veering toward climate crisis. *As the Globe Warms* is not without gadgetry and new media—I use a camera and screen to depict web-cam life and the work itself, as well as being onstage, has online forms of audio and video novels.

But by bucking ready-to-consume categories, I hope to contribute to a new paradigm of sustainable culture that I see rippling out in the arts and elsewhere. With a minimum of resources, without mass-culture/high-culture approval, we can now send ripples from a backwater that can potentially spread out and join forces with other currents in the common cultural stream as never before. Why not take theatre, even as it is being made, directly to the heart of our subject matter—to the people in the trenches about whom we imagine dialogue and initiate actual conversations, no matter how uncomfortable? I envision productions that can reflect this process: marrying bare bones, minimalist means to a maximal engagement of time, imagination and social inclusion, and articulate an ethos of sustainability, a "slow theatre" analogous to the slow food movement.

Imagine my pleasure in discovering that the great Australian art critic Robert Hughes had this idea too, way before I did:

"What we need more of is slow art: art that holds time as a vase holds water: art that grows out of modes of perception and whose skill and doggedness make you think and feel; art that isn't merely sensational, that doesn't get its message across in 10 seconds, that isn't falsely iconic, that hooks onto something deep-running in our natures. In a word, art that is the very opposite of mass media. For no spiritually authentic art can beat mass media at their own game." [9]

Amen, brother.

"Stand-up novelist" **Heather Woodbury** is known for novel-sized solo works that combine serial storytelling with high-wire performance. *What Ever,* her 1990s stage tour-de-force, was broadcast on radio, with host Ira Glass, and published by Farrar, Straus & Giroux. Her current serial *As the Globe Warms* is a podcast serial on *heatherwoodbury.com.*

[9] *http://www.theguardian.com/artanddesign/2004/jun/03/art,* In a speech delivered at Burlington House, London, England. Published in *The Guardian.* [accessed 16 February 2015]

CONCURRENCIES

Aaron Landsman

1. Form

Most of the time I don't know what I am doing, until it's living in the room. Except that most of the things I have done—as a maker, performer or viewer—I have done within the genre of experimental theater. And I've been doing these things for long enough that what I make inevitably ends up sharing a lot of its DNA with that form.

But ultimately, I don't really care whether you think what I made for you is theater, performance art, social practice or something on the border of art and non-art. What difference does it make? Can you take in the experience on the experience's terms, without predetermining what it is supposed to be? I'd love it if you could.

I know that making my project *City Council Meeting*—which, depending on the day, has felt like a bold step forward, a failed social experiment, a devised documentary theater work with audience participation, or a case of Emperor's New Clothes—has transformed me as an artist in some way. It has become less important how what I do fits or doesn't into a particular genre. Is that innovative of me? Or just careless.

Created in collaboration with director Mallory Catlett, and designer Jim Findlay, *City Council Meeting* involves found and original text, a set of instructions and prompts, and live and recorded video. The project is about the forms through which we govern ourselves locally. It's performed by the audience with the help of staffers, some of whom are actors, and some of whom are not. It is a combination of a touring production and a community work we build locally in each city where it's presented. Depending on who you talk to, it's either difficult to get through, or entirely accessible, even fun. It is procedural and non-narrative. It is meant to be able to exist almost anywhere but a black-box. Is it theater? I don't know.

2. Craft

Maybe it helps to anchor this nebulous term 'innovation' by thinking about craft and technique. As an actor, I am a huge fan of the cliché that says that in order to be in the moment onstage, we have to leave technique backstage. We have to learn something well enough to forget it. Whether I am in a naturalistic scene that calls for particular, scripted emotional highs and lows, in a clown piece where I am supposed to embody immense guilelessness, or in an ensemble work that is about just listening to the other human beings with whom I am onstage, I know the common thread is that I need to have honed what I know well enough to abandon it.

Is there an equivalent for authors? Meaning, as a writer, what do I gain by worrying about whether or not what I am making is theater? What does that worry inhibit me from doing? Is it possible to trust the long years of working and watching, teaching and listening, to let the process determine the form? And if so, where do you locate the rigor? Is it possible to let the motivation or form remain a mystery until the last possible moment, trusting that the hundred other projects you've worked on, the failures and successes alike, are all feeding into the possibilities of the current process?

3. Production

When I think about form and craft, I also can't help but think of how the work gets produced, because certain ways of producing yield certain kinds of work.

We made *City Council Meeting* through a three-year residency at HERE, in New York. We developed the piece through additional residencies in two other cities, through NPN support at DiverseWorks in Houston, and through a community residency with ASU Gammage. Those three years allowed us to build a piece through multiple, fully-produced work-in-progress showings, lots of trial and (lots of) error, and concurrent efforts at fundraising and presenter cultivation. Since then we've honed the process to bring it to Zspace in San Francisco, and Keene State College's Redfern Arts Center in New Hampshire.

And we're working on a book and an educational curriculum based on the show, too.

HERE took on the project when it was nothing more than an idea on a page. Gammage committed to it in order to spark a longer conversation among its audience and among performing artists in Phoenix/Tempe, about the form of theater and the form of politics; before the curtain went up on *City Council Meeting* there this February, they had already decided to continue that conversation with me through new projects. DiverseWorks drew on our several-year history of working together to expand a conversation that already existed there.

All three of these producing partners embedded themselves in something ongoing and put resources toward the unknown. Whether that is innovative or not, it's certainly not an easy sell for presenters. Though HERE sometimes raised objections to how we wanted the project to evolve, we managed to stick together and make something, albeit quite different than what I proposed to them. It was performed in different spaces than we expected, performed by different people.

At our best, we all balanced ourselves among the needs of the project, the evolving process and the visions of all the partners. It felt less hierarchical than many processes I've been involved in, regardless of the fact that, technically speaking, I was the artist, and they were the institution, giving me an opportunity I could not really have without them. In practice the piece became something much wilder and more unruly than it could have been if it had been mapped out on paper and achieved according to plan.

4. Audience

When people say "theater is a collaborative art form" they usually mean what happens onstage is created collaboratively, among artists. I want to talk about the collaboration between artists and audiences. Abigail Browde and Michael Silverstone, co-directors of the group 600 Highwaymen told me recently that they look for ways to insert gaps in their work, where the audience must insert themselves as co-authors. I love this, and I wonder how early that co-authorship can begin? How are we inviting people into the room with us, into the conversation? How can we honor our dependency on our viewers, not just to buy tickets, but to enter our spaces and projects in a well-articulated, well-lived way? How can we make better invitations?

One sure thing I came away with from the recent run of *City Council Meeting* in New York was that the piece is not for everyone. Just as certain, you'd be more likely to get it if you were brought into it in a way that made you feel like you belonged there. Maybe we walked you around Jim's set and showed you a bit of the video for a few minutes, along with your classmates; maybe you heard or read an interview beforehand; maybe you came with a group, or with someone who'd seen it before. What if the art includes school performances, introductions, roundtable conversations, multiple viewings and orientations? When does the "performance" start?

This is tricky because we don't want our show to be beholden to program notes or ancillary activities. But for some work, maybe it's necessary to think the performance begins at the moment of invitation, and that it's incumbent on us to curate how everyone gets in the room, just like we dramaturg what happens onstage.

Does this mean we should assume that our work is only for a select audience, who must be prepared in advance? Well, no and yes.

No, because anyone who wants to come should be able to, and some people can just dive right in. But yes because don't we inadvertently curate our audiences already? We do it by the prices we charge for tickets, by who sees people like them on stage, in a range of possible roles, or with them in the audience, and therefore feels welcomed. We do it by who we ask to run our institutions. By how much money we offer to pay people. We do it by our choice of material, and by the gradual inculcation (or not) of people into our forms and behaviors. There are already such class, racial and cultural biases embedded in the way in which theater is presented, packaged and sold. I'd like to advocate we open up *that* conversation as we talk about innovation.

I am an avid formal experimentalist. I believe in trying something simply because it appeals to you, because you want to challenge common assumptions about what is possible or not possible. I think it's totally awesome and necessary to make work for a very small viewership, as well as for a large one.

I also know that everything we do carries a politics with it, and a message. Form is content, to some degree. The postcard is content. The website is content. Who is in the room with us is content. They are inextricably linked.

I think what I am advocating here is that we engage some basic questions: What are we doing and why? Who is in the room and how did we all get here? You don't have to know any answers until after closing night. But if we do answer, broadly and deeply, and also specifically enough, can we innovate from inside the process itself?

Aaron Landsman is a playwright, actor and teacher. His work is often staged in the places people perform their lives: offices, homes, meeting rooms, vehicles. Recent projects include *City Council Meeting*, *Appointment*, *Running Away From The One With The Knife* and *Empathy School*. He is a 2014-16 Princeton Arts Fellow and the 2013-16 ASU Gammage Artist in Residence. He lives in New York City. *www.citycouncilmeeting.org*

TAKING CONTROL OF THE NARRATIVE

E. M. Lewis

All my characters are trying to wrestle the narrative away from each other right now. When it first happened, when I was working on *True Story*, it was disconcerting, kind of shocking and violent, really, but I went with it. And I doubted myself, because... well, who doesn't, but I trusted the voices and followed them out into the deep, dark places, because I've really begun to understand, these last few years, that that's the only way to do it.

It's been a nice couple of years. I got a fellowship, and then another fellowship, so I quit my sensible day job and moved across the country, far away from everything I know, and my family, to New Jersey (!), and have been writing full time. And it's been nice. It's been... Madeleine L'Engle used this word "deepening" in one of her books, and that's how I've felt, like I've been deepening, finding my true voice in a way that I've never—

(How am I going to pay the rent this month?)

—come so close to doing before. And I've been writing so much more than I ever ever have. New full lengths, and short plays, and a one-man show that cut so close to the bone I pretty much had a panic attack when we read it in workshop. Maybe not a full panic attack. I don't know, I've never had one before. But all of a sudden my heart started pounding so loud I couldn't hear Stephen reading anymore. But then I could hear again after a while, and I stayed really quiet there in my chair, and I don't think anybody noticed. You're not supposed to talk during the response period anyway, so I—

(don't know how I'm going to keep doing this. I'm 42 years old, and what the fuck do I have to show for it? no husband, no kids, no house, no—is this a mid-life crisis? How fucking trite that would be. Jesus.)

[why is my internal voice so profane when I never swear?]

—shut up and listened. Is it a good sign when you give yourself a panic attack from something you wrote? It's probably not a sign at all. But it was a hard play to write. It's about guns and gun control.

Not really.

It's about me and my husband, and how he died.

Which makes it really no different from any of my plays, which are all about me and my husband and how he died, except the rest of them cleverly call all the characters by different names and are set in different places, so I don't think people realize that they're all about us, that I've been writing about us all this time.

It's called *The Gun Show*. It's the first thing I've written in first person in a long time. It's written for a guy to read, but he's playing me, and at a couple points during the play, he points a flashlight at me, picking me out of the audience so they know I'm there and they can identify the guilty party, the one who wrote this thing, the one who... I took out the puppet. There used to be a puppet, and I used to have lines, talking back to the actor who is playing me, but I took them out, because it was already in there, in the text, everything I needed. And I put a clause in the notes about some time, maybe, I'll be brave enough to read it myself, but that's probably bullshit. I don't know. Maybe I'll do it. Maybe I want to wrestle the narrative away from my actors and claim my own words. Maybe I want to confess my sins.

(maybe I should move back home to the farm in Oregon)

[you're gonna have to do something if you can't pay your rent this month]

Into the woods. It's a good metaphor. It was good back in fairy tale days, with all the romance and darkness, and it's even better after Mr. Sondheim mucked about with it, because he added the complicatedness that we've all run up against, and said, "Yeah, the woods is that, too." I just saw the show the other day, over at the McCarter, and the lyrics have been sounding in my head like a bell.

"Sometimes people leave you, halfway through the wood."

(Yeah.)

"Nothing's quite so clear, now. Feel you've lost your way?"

(Yeah.)

But I'm getting closer to something as an artist, I think.

(Is that bullshit? That sounds dangerously close to—)

Those terrible true things. The small personal true things and the larger global true things. I feel like I'm getting closer—

(But how do you ever know? Some people like my plays, I've had some productions and such, but how do I know if any of this means anything? If it's the right path? Maybe I should have—)

[—been a helicopter nurse. I know that sounds like a radical notion, but there was a moment, back when I was at Chemeketa Community College, when I was nineteen, when I seriously considered it. Flying around and saving people. What's not to like?]

(—done something different with my life, gone down a surer path.)

[What's surer?]

{Accounting?}

[I'd be a terrible accountant. I can't even calculate the tip properly.]

(There has to be something surer than this.)

[Is that even a word? Surer?]

I could die tomorrow.

(I really could. It's been ages since I had health insurance. Looking both ways at the intersections only gets you so far.)

At a certain point... at this point, I guess... you start to ask yourself, is it worthwhile, what I've done with my life, what I'm doing with my life? What do I have to show for my life?

(The job hunt hasn't been going well. I don't need much, but I need something. I'll mow lawns. I'll wash windows. I'm not too proud to do anything, but I can't even get a call back on most of the jobs I'm applying for. What am I doing wrong? Or does the economy still just suck this bad? Maybe it's just that nobody wants me.)

[Fuck 'em. Fuck 'em all. You're a playwright, goddamn it, you shouldn't be washing fucking windows, you should be writing plays.]

{easy to say, but then maybe when you get back from that play festival in Fayetteville you find all your stuff out on the lawn and they've changed the locks on you, and there's no power outlet for your laptop out on the lawn, girlie-girl.}

(Sometimes I'm terrified, sometimes I lie in the dark and wonder what the fuck I'm doing—)

[—but that's okay, because you're a writer, if you weren't fucked up what the fuck would you write about?]

{yeah, tell yourself that}

(Do you lie in the dark and wonder what the fuck you're doing sometimes?)

Stop, already! Just stop!!!

(A moment. A Pinter pause.)

This is me, trying to take control of the narrative. The writing narrative and the life narrative. And realizing that you never can, and you always have to keep trying, and you always have to keep trying, and you never can.

There is no "surer" thing than this. Nothing is sure. And we have to figure out why we should push the rock up the hill anyway, and how, and if we can keep a roof over our heads while we're doing it.

This essay was supposed to be about artistic innovation, but I'm writing about my rent money instead. Because they are inextricable from one another. Both require all of our courage and all of our humility.

I don't just want to be a braver writer, after all.

I want to be a braver person.

Here's a funny story. I got an email from someone I didn't know the other day. The woman said that she'd come across my play *The Edge of Ross Island* on her way to Staunton, and thought it was really interesting. I emailed her back, thanking her for saying so. And I asked her where she'd "come across it," because... that was a funny way to put it. And it turns out she'd found it on the sidewalk. Laying there on the sidewalk in Staunton, Virginia, for no apparent reason, and she bent down and picked it up, and read it, and in her second email, where she told me all this, she said that she couldn't put it down.

Something about that whole story makes me laugh, and makes me want to keep going.

Oh, world!

Courage, I guess, is the word I've been looking for.

I want to keep writing more courageously and living more courageously. Whether I do that in New Jersey or Oregon, while washing windows or making plays, while voicing my own words or asking actors to do it for me.

The boldest innovations came from people who acted bravely. I want to be brave.

("Things will come out right now. We can make it so.")

Be brave.

E. M. Lewis is an award-winning playwright and librettist. Winner: Steinberg Award for *Song of Extinction*; Primus Prize for *Heads*, American Theater Critics Association; Hodder Fellowship, Princeton University. Her work has been produced around the world, and published by Samuel French. She lives in Oregon. Member: Dramatists Guild. *www.emlewisplaywright.com*

IF SOMEONE CALLS MY NAME

Zac Kline

Innovation says yes.

Innovation looks you straight in the eye and says:
"How do you do? Would you like to get in? Let's go for a ride."

I asked a longtime director colleague what she thinks excites me in the theatre?
She responded: "Weird things, like Ivo Van Hove." It's true, I do have a strong penchant for, and feel a strong connection to the Belgium-born, Amsterdam-based director's work.
But the question is, why?

The answer, his work and the work of Toneelgroep Amsterdam does something and goes somewhere I as an audience member have not been before. The ferocity of an animal on stage—literally and figuratively *Teorema*, the deafening muteness of war in a modern landscape in *Roman Tragedies* and the heartbreakingly transfixing mix of art, life, love, loss and memory in *The Opening Night*.

Being innovative means being aggressive and Van Hove is surely aggressive, and not just the physical grappling (or food fights) he places on stage. He's aggressive with his intent. Aggressive with the knowledge that in order for theatre to do something, to feel like something and make us feel something, it cannot just spar—and a lot of theatre does —but has to actually land a knockout punch.

Innovative theatre is a workout. Innovative theatre makes your heart race and your body jump.

Cock did that. Mike Bartlett's superb play about fluid sexuality was directed by James MacDonald (in its New York production) with an energy, smoothness and precision that made it feel like this story—one that boils down to love, hurt and people who need each other—was being told for the very first time. Each cut of the dramatic razor, small or large, bled anew.

It's hard to capture innovation in a bottle. It is of course being there, but also being there and letting it in. *Here Lies Love* (recently at the Public Theater and National Theatre in London), is a remarkable piece of theatre, not necessarily just because of the story it tells or how the story is written, but because of the commitment it makes to itself and to its audience. David Byrne, Fatboy Slim and Alex Timbers have created a disco Wikipedia (and I mean that as a pure compliment) of the life of Imelda Marcos, a play in a dance club/a dance club in a play and in doing so they have wrought an innovative piece of theatre, because, they invite—no—demand that the audience participate.

We do not witness history, we participate in it. *Here Lies Love* understands this. It has the audience dancing, we are complicit with history, its rights and its many wrongs before we even realize what we are doing. We dance with the (fictionalized yet real life) heroes, the villains, the in-betweens, we just dance. It is theatre that does not let us watch, but activates us.

In a blink of an eye I was caught up in the sound and the sex of politics before I could take stock of the injustices being perpetrated again-and-again. My heart was racing and I had fallen in love. Innovation is falling in love.

When the lights came up at the end of *Here Lies Love* my wife, who attended the show with me, commented that she was not jarred back into reality with an overwhelming sense that she had stayed at the club too long, instead, for a moment she felt like the disco lights were now the reality, and this other space is not where she wanted to be. I too wanted to be back in the holy and broken space of living, breathing theatre.

I often ask my playwriting students, many of whom are still in high school what would they like to see on stage that would truly excite them? The last time I asked, one student replied: "If someone said my name." There is something beautiful in the statement. Because it is what we're all asking for in a way when we enter the theatre and what we are striving for as theatremakers.

Here Lies Love said my name, so did Mike Bartlett's *Cock*, so do the theatre productions of Ivo Van Hove, as do so many others.

And so I am left to question and left with a challenge for my colleagues, my collaborators and most importantly for myself:

Will I be innovative?
Will I say yes?
Will mine say yours?

Zac Kline is a New York-based playwright. He is a contributing author and co-editor of *24 Gun Control Plays* along with Caridad Svich. His play in the collection *What are we going to do about little brother?* has been read and performed across the United States. He is the co-artistic director of Missing Bolts Productions along with Blair Baker. For more information please visit *www.missingbolts.com*.

VIOLENCE AND THEATRE-MAKING

John Moletress

"Art is violent. To be decisive is violent."
—Anne Bogart, *A Director Prepares: Seven Essays on Art and Theatre*

October 2014, Berlin. On tour performing *JARMAN (all this maddening beauty)*, an on-going solo performance collaboration with Caridad Svich and force/collision, I took a pit stop in the city to rediscover my romance with it. I had not been since 1997. Call it youth, call it curiosity, call it a love for ambitious architecture and imagined spaces, my infatuation with Berlin runs deep. Endless seeing. Endless ways to get lost and caught up in the geography of steel cranes and buildings teetering on the edge between now and then. It is a world of violence, separation, fierce character and ultimately, radical redemption.

Unless we've been to the Staatliche Museum in Berlin
And seen it up close.
—Caridad Svich, *JARMAN (all this maddening beauty)*

Svich writes the words of the young artist in *JARMAN*, daring my inner artist to go out and find the subject at the center of the play, Saint Sebastian. I take the S-Bahn to the Potsdamer Platz and walk a bit to the Staatliche. Weaving my way through the corridors and ancient scenes of Christian heroics, cherubs cut against sky blue clouds and faces both pallid and rose colored against varying spectrums of light, the agony and ecstasy of 500 years of European painting overwhelms me. Sandro Botticelli's saint appears. Tethered to wood and immortalized with tempera on canvas, he hangs upon the wall which hangs upon the structure of the entirety of the Gemäldegalerie. The saint is smaller than I had imagined. Fantastical imagination cannot be measured by metrics. He looks fragile, as if breath might blow him from his position, turning canvas to dust and retreating into memory. He is beautiful. The arrows enter him beautifully. Hedda Gabbler once said of death, "do it beautifully."

JARMAN (all this maddening beauty) is a performative gesture inspired by the late artist, activist, writer, filmmaker and gardener Derek Jarman. The production orientates itself to both present and past, gazing upon the icon through imagined territories and constructed spaces. By looking back, the lens becomes reflective. In one scene, the young artist sits in the dark of the cinema watching Jarman's 1976 film *Sebastiane* for the first time and his experience of the world expands into vibrant colors and thoughts not unlike my imagining of Botticelli's saint. The violence of abandoned censorship and fierce sexuality rages across the screen. Violence and art. Queerness and the subversive.

In society violence too often takes the form of coercion, exerting force with the intention of harm. Violence is a cycle. It bears down onto a spinning wheel, repeating actions over and over again. On the other hand there is art where the violent act sparks a shifting paradigm, creating new materials and new models for making work. The initial movement towards art-making is to make change on a molecular level. In painting, the violent act is the first stroke upon the canvas. In writing, the first word. In ensemble theatre making, the violent act is stepping away from table work and moving freely about the space. It is this type of creative violence that the world needs.

To perform trust is an act of violence against our physical space, our sphere of individuality. This sphere can exist in a constant state of fluctuation, growing larger or smaller depending on external circumstances, cultural conditions or social context. As civilians, this trust can be violently infringed upon. The information we receive and how we receive it may influence our ability to trust by drastic measure. Such can be seen time and time again by traumatic events and the proceeding response. Fight or flight sets in until we are informed we can feel safe again. There is no safety in art. Materials pour out onto the canvas and can only be made null by destruction.

As theatre artists, we are asked to perform in a hierarchy of trust. We trust the stage manager will inform us of the correct rehearsal time. We trust the director will lead us down the most truthful path. We trust our fellow actors will not betray us in the moment. There is theatre that causes a visceral reaction, whether through content or form or a combination of both. This type of theatre stops us. We want it to spark dialogue. So often in our daily lives we quickly move between points, tasks, engagements in order that by the end of the day we may resume our time as autonomous individuals. To stop, to think, to reflect becomes a violent act, a cessation of movement.

As in the case of creating a new work, the period of development seems inadequate. The dialogue can always go further and mine the material a bit deeper. We are thinkers. However as performers, we must negotiate between our thinking minds and our moving bodies. Once we give ourselves permission to let go and allow for the fact of failure, we can begin again.

John Moletress in *JARMAN (all this maddening beauty)*, Dance Place, Washington D.C. Photo by David Dowling.

I founded force/collision, an interdisciplinary performance ensemble based in Washington, D.C. so that we might have a lab for creating new work and exploring ways of working. We come together on a regular basis to discuss, to move, to strengthen our vocabulary for making work. Our long periods of project development can be both a blessing and a curse. When the time comes to stage, it can seem disruptive. Gathering the material and shaping it for presentation can be a daunting task. One move may feel right while twenty others feel ill-fitting. Having also worked in the regional theatre model with four weeks of rehearsal, there is something to be said about creating under the pressure of time. I strive to trust initial impulses but it is easy to lose steam and get caught up in thinking and re-thinking over a period of time. Structure is key.

Lately with force/collision, we are approaching our work broadly at first, developing the movement vocabulary, adding text and thinking dramaturgically after we have laid the foundation. Mostly, we work with source material and experimental texts that are characters themselves, the embodiment of a language to be written over the signs and symbols of the performer's gestural vocabulary. If the addition of text seems too sudden, too premature, we return to simply moving and responding.

The question of theatrical innovation in America and the development of new work radiates out from a place of mobility. How do we move forward and with what tools? Language is ever-present. Under changing systems, meanings, symbols and our relationship to the functionality of language is mobile. Plays become re-energized by evolving contexts. To innovate is to become hyper-aware, to become more present. Spoken language does not seem enough, so we must pay close attention to how we speak and with what intent. The definition of innovation–to invent, to introduce something new–seems deceiving in theatre. If we look at innovation as a means to re-shape, to re-investigate or to pose a new way of looking we may feel less overwhelmed. "Necessity is the mother of invention." It is from our necessity to respond and create, as long as we remain openly aware, that innovation will present itself.

John Moletress is a multi-disciplined artist, university professor and Founding Director of force/collision, an interdisciplinary performance ensemble based in Washington, D.C. BA Muhlenberg College; MFA George Washington University. *JohnMoletress.com; force-collision.org*

BEYOND THE
"DEAD PLAYWRIGHT" APPROACH

Mariana Carreño King

"I like working with dead playwrights," a director once told a playwright whose play he was directing. The implication was clear: shut up and get out of my rehearsal; your job is done and now let me do mine.

Reinventing plays as a director is obviously a valid form of artistic expression. How many Shakespeare adaptations in all sorts of settings have we seen, from Joe Papp's *Naked Hamlet* to the Reduced Shakespeare Company production of *The Compleat Works of Wllm Shkspr?* And living playwrights adapt "dead playwrights" all the time too: Luis Alfaro's brilliant *Oedipus el Rey* and *Electricidad*, Migdalia Cruz's *Hamlet*, Caridad Svich's *12 Ophelias* and *Iphigenia Crash Land Falls on the Neon Shell That Was Once Her Heart*, or José Rivera's *Sueños* based on Calderón de la Barca's *Life is a Dream* come to mind.

But directors working on new work who prefer the "dead playwright" approach are missing out on the innovation achieved by true collaborations. The dialogue that goes on when everybody digs into the work, discovers new meanings and contributes to the creation of a new play.

And often, directors who prefer the "dead playwright" approach also like their actors pretty dead too: they are rarely interested in the work actors do to deepen their understanding of the characters, their emotional lives. They are more interested in how the play "looks".

Again, there's nothing necessarily wrong with this approach, and some directors have achieved incredible work this way—moving and beautiful to watch. I just think they're missing out, or at least not taking advantage of the different points of view that a play can provoke.

Beyond the director and the actors, what a privilege to have the whole artistic team in the rehearsal room. A sound designer to figure out what to underscore or to suggest ideas that a director alone might never come up with. The same goes for set and lighting and costume designers who contribute enormously to create the magical world we all want to inhabit.

Of course that's difficult, especially in the real world of off- and off-off-Broadway theatre in New York, where the money is short and everything is driven by results. We need to get going: three weeks rehearsal, one week tech, previews and boom, done. Go home and write something new. Put pretty pictures in your portfolio and move on to the next interview. Audition for your next project. Theatre is ephemeral by nature and you have to move on.

But there are other ways to create new work. Pina Bausch and Robert Lepage are great examples of the importance of collaboration, of absorbing what different artists bring to the table (or the stage) to create magical worlds. They can (Bausch could) afford long processes that involve multiple countries and disciplines, and it's worth noting that neither Tanztheater (Bausch) nor Ex Machina (Lepage) are based in the United States, where support for the arts keeps dwindling.

Bausch and Lepage are in a class of their own, but we can still learn from them. We can learn to listen and observe and absorb. We can learn to be open to the different opinions and techniques and disciplines of everybody in the room. Even with limited resources and time, we can strive to feed each other's imaginations, to check our egos at the door and pay attention to the world around us. We live in a diverse, crazy world, and we do not always take advantage of it. We're blinded by our own limitations and prejudices, real and imagined.

There are many obstacles: the corporatization of theatre, risk-averse producers, lack of resources, the homogenization of culture in general. Women and artists of color have it even harder. It is a little depressing out there. But we can still try and help each other along the way. Listen to each other and not just keep yelling. Welcome more people into the room and not just shut the door.

Sure, we can learn a lot by reinventing dead playwrights, by honoring our ancestors. But there's nothing like working with the living: multi-cultural, multi-disciplinary artists that push boundaries and create entirely new worlds that we can all inhabit, if only for a fleeting moment.

Mariana Carreño King is a writer, director and translator. Her plays have been developed at Mabou Mines, INTAR, Labyrinth Theatre Company, Public Theatre and The Lark, among others. Her play *The Prisoner* won the 2014 MetLife National Playwriting Competition. As a director she has worked at INTAR, Stages Repertory (Houston, TX), Iati Theatre and The Lark, among others.

ACT FOUR

AT PLAY

AN EDUCATED GAMBLE

Daniel Gallant

What is innovation? Intelligent persistence. An educated gamble. When the gamble fails, an innovator learns why and gambles smarter the next time.

In 2002, I was between jobs and rebounding from an ACL tear. I wandered into an event at a side-street venue on the Upper West Side. The building was eclectic, quirky and full of possibility. I learned that live music filled the venue, but no theater events were held there. A sleek space with lighting grid and soundboard, box office and bar—so why no theater? I asked if I could stage a festival. Management said, "Sure," as long as I required no pay, staff, office or publicity. I was 26 and broke; I'm sure they thought I'd fade away. But I dove in. A cashless "yes" is catnip to a hungry young producer.

Management expected harmless plays by local scribes. I called up Wendy Wasserstein. Didn't know her, just thought: Worst case, she'll say no. But Wendy volunteered to talk onstage about her craft and Pulitzer-winning career. She saw value in our fledgling festival, in part because we soldiered fearlessly without a budget.

We launched short-play marathons, musical theater series and Shakespeare classes. The festival grew into a full-fledged theater program, and other artists we approached neglected to say no: Norman Mailer, Tony Kushner, Craig Lucas, Liz Swados, Neil LaBute, Warren Leight, Chazz Palminteri, plus rising playwrights (like Jason Grote and Dmitry Lipkin) who have since achieved success.

Plenty of artists declined our invitations; every time a guest said "no," I adjusted my approach and my criteria. Conventional wisdom should have dissuaded us from pursuing big-name talent, since we had scarce money or collateral to offer—but the artists were gracious, and excited to have a grassroots outlet for new work and conversation.

At some point, management offered me a salary, and at some point, the quirky venue became part of the 92nd Street Y. Those two changes did not impact my core strategy: pursue top talent, create compelling events and promote aggressively to the press, stretch (but never break) the budget. If the budget is zero, focus on dialogue rather than costumes.

There were plentiful misfires and failed steps along the way, and I often worried that I had taken the wrong path. But the path only makes sense when you look back at it from a higher elevation. To innovate, you have to learn what doesn't work, adjust, and then try again. Know what your resources (time, sweat, cash, reputation, friendships) can buy you. Stretch your dollar, but don't lose your shirt. Artists and arts managers always lack sufficient resources—we are, by our nature and professions, in a perpetual state of want. But "want" and "lack" are priceless resources that keep us gunning for success.

Some arts institutions spend more resources to propagate their own bureaucracy than to create new art. And yes, the mechanism must survive, the amoeba must continue, art requires infrastructure. But the edgy and experimental spirit that generates compelling new work is fueled by proximity to hunger and risk. Some large arts entities forget the necessary hustle that drives innovation—and the smaller arts entities to which hunger and improvisation come naturally are often most at risk of disappearing. It isn't easy to maintain conditions that are friendly to innovation. But—for the sake of artists and their audience—we must try.

Daniel Gallant is the Executive Director of the Nuyorican Poets Cafe. He previously served as the Director of Theater and Talk Programming at the 92nd Street Y's Makor Center and at 92YTribeca. His work has been featured in the *Wall Street Journal*, the *New York Times*, *Crain's New York*, *Time Out New York*, the *Huffington Post*, the *Daily News*, the *New York Post* and other periodicals, and he has appeared in shows on MTV, NBC, NY1, Univision, Telemundo, CBS, the BBC and other networks (including a recent appearance on MTV's show "Washington Heights").

THE ESSENTIALITY OF INNOVATION

Daniel Brunet

In 2006, while translating an excerpt of an essay on theater and economy by German dramaturg Carl Hegemann for a month-long simulation of a German state theater (financed by the German Federal Ministry of Economics and Labor with funds directly descended from the Marshall Plan) at HERE Arts Center in New York, I was struck by the undeniable truth of one of his primary observations. From an economic standpoint, theater is a staggeringly inefficient medium. As I began to consider the implications of this statement and contemplate the vast amounts of coordination, collaboration and creative energy required to realize even the "simplest" piece of theater–by definition existing for a finite period of time and limited to a finite number of spectators–I found it nearly impossible to conceive of "efficient" theater within this context. And yet outside of this context theater is more "efficient" than nearly any other form in providing a specific community a place to examine its shared history and narrative–regardless of the average economic return on investment.

Another example of heavily subsidized German artistic experimentation can be found in the key figures of *Unendlicher Spaß (Infinite Jest)*, Hebbel am Ufer's glorious million-euro paean to David Foster Wallace and outgoing artistic director Matthias Lilienthal in 2012, a twenty-four-hour durational performance moving by bus through eight locations in the former West Berlin and featuring 12 different pieces devised by 12 different groups exploring various themes surrounding the author, his work and the city the performance took place in. Performed eight times for a maximum of 150 audience members with a maximum ticket price of 50 euros, selling every single ticket for every single performance at the highest possible ticket price could theoretically bring in 60,000 euros—that is, six percent of the total costs.

From a traditional capitalist understanding of business and efficiency, this production could only be seen as a loss-making enterprise. Its monetary income failed, on an epic scale, to match, let alone exceed its monetary expenditures. Yet, as the project's sponsorship by Germany's Federal Cultural Foundation (which alone contributed just shy of 500,000 euros) clearly demonstrates, the cultural officials and professional juries responsible for assessing the quality of the artistic innovation of these economically untenable undertakings found the work to be worthy and to contain an added value not quantifiable in euros and cents.

Indeed, ever since Hegemann highlighted for me the precarious practice of applying the same term to very different fields, in this case, culture and business, I find myself regularly noting phrases that have forced their way to the forefront of the momentary vernacular and that are applied universally, with a one size fits all mentality—regardless of whether one term can have the same meaning in nearly diametrically opposed contexts.

Perhaps this has always been the case; perhaps the long, strange trip of globalization, digitization and moving from the Print Age to the Digital Age has exacerbated this practice as the world walks a tightrope between the stunning diversity made possible by the free flow of information and the risk of stupefying homogeneity as the entire planet increasingly consumes identical cultural and business commodities.

At any rate, the application of a concept like "efficient," "sustainable" or even "economic" will yield radically different results based upon the field and practice in question. "Innovation," on the other hand, achieves a nearly identical result in nearly every context.

As defined by *Merriam-Webster*, the intransitive verb "innovate" designates the act of "making changes" or "doing something in a new way." In this basic formulation, the verb also seems to carry an inherently positive connotation—rare is the usage of innovation to denote a negative change. Within this formulation, I also feel myself forced to read a certain method within the madness in question, if you will—that the "innovation" is a carefully calculated contribution to an existing process or entity designed to make it better—not to simply effect change for change's sake.

In fields as opposed as business and art (ignoring, of course, their shared child, the "entertainment industry"), I find it curious that "innovation" is used so frequently and so singularly, that the abstract principle is so highly and universally valued that it alone can be used to sell products and attract subsidies. In a certain sense, "innovation" seems like good old-fashioned common sense, something that should be self-evident in nearly every field, a continual improvement process, a constant reinvention, an ongoing adjustment to changing facts on the ground and perspectives.

In order to retain its relevance and power, art must constantly adapt to altered circumstances and ripples in the zeitgeist. In the same way, any business subjected to competition that does not maintain a maximum degree of flexibility and a willingness to constantly improve will soon lose out.

When I consider theater as a social and political tool used by a specific community to examine and question its own stories, narratives and perceptions, innovation is absolutely essential. Just as human beings and communities of human beings are constantly changing, ever mutable and in a continuous state of flux, so must be the methodologies and practices applied to the creation of the tool that allows this reflection.

Still, barely more than a century after the invention of the moving picture, sixty years after the television has become a fixture in almost every home (in all parts of the world) and just about two decades into the ubiquity of the Internet, theater has been forced to compete increasingly for increasingly fragmented attention spans and to insist upon convocation at a certain time in a certain place in order to convene and commune over an ephemeral experience. These circumstances serve only to accelerate the inherent innovation in a constant pursuit of essentiality.

Indeed, from an economic standpoint, theater is truly an "inefficient" model—and yet one that is absolutely essential and one unequivocally greater than the sum of its parts, as its continued existence and the unbridled passion of its practitioners and spectators clearly attests. There is an added value to theater that makes an argument focusing solely on profit margins and yield inherently flawed. And it is this built-in process of innovation that accompanies all immediate art that relentlessly drives forward the pursuit of the new, the adaptation to changing circumstances and the necessity of being firmly and undeniably essential.

Daniel Brunet is the Producing Artistic Director of English Theatre Berlin|International Performing Arts Center. A theater maker and translator, his directorial work and translations have been presented internationally and his translations and essays have been published in *PEN America, The Mercurian, Asymptote, Theater, TheatreForum, Contemporary Theatre Review* and *alt.theatre*. He is the recipient of a Fulbright grant as well as a grant from the PEN Translation Fund and a Literature Fellowship in Translation from the National Endowment of the Arts.

AGAINST MASTERY

David Herskovits

Over the past many years I have developed a variety of techniques in what I have come to call "forced failure." Essentially these are strategies that force the performer to fail by setting an impossible task, and the failure itself generates the material that I really prize: the by-product is the product, to put it in a target/margin way, and we succeed through failure. I should add that the practice might involve not only performers, but other partners: designers, technicians, dramaturgs, producers, musicians and assistants—really anyone invested in the work.

This can be done in endless ways. Typically, there is a speech, or a scene, or a passage of dialogue, or a part of a story that needs to be expressed. I demand that the people involved express it, but then I limit the process such that they are doomed to fail, and they have to reinvent whatever the thing may be. In these cases there is a pretext of some kind, a play usually, although it could also be a scenario or a fable, historical sources, non-dramatic literature, or just an idea we develop together. Usually the outcome of this first step is recorded in some way. Inevitably that recording itself fails (it is distorted, flawed, wrong), and it in turn sponsors another iteration. For example: demand that the performer learn a speech, but give them insufficient time, then as they attempt to say the speech record that; so all the little glitches and passages—"ohhhh... [long pause]... totally blank....or not, or not, that's it or not to be!"—are captured; then transcribe that and commit to it with exact fidelity. It becomes the new score. Or the speech could be transcribed by another actor by hand, without stopping or explanation; that transcription must be read by another person who of course cannot decipher the handwriting and has to supply gaps as best she or he can. Two or more people could be given some time to read and work on a scene, which I demand they stage, by which I mean create a movement score that is precise and repeatable. Then of course they must perform it exactly and without stopping. This yields a physical failure, as the movement is garbled, elided and re-improvised while retaining nonetheless some memory of its nonexistent original (you could call that "original" an intention). Phases of recording, either by hand or audio recording or even video recording are usually an important part of the process, as capturing what happens ("the music of what happens," in Seamus Heaney's lovely phrase) is so important. The point of course is to create things we could never have dreamed or envisioned if we had planned them. The point is to sidestep trying to envision the work, to let go of interpretive ideas, and above all to stop thinking. The point is to break the dead hand of mastery.

We work so hard to feel mastery of our métier; we trumpet our competence and artistry and importance loud in the noisy uncaring amphitheater of American culture because no one else gives a damn and if anything their disregard reminds us how trivial our own work is in the scheme of things. We crown ourselves. No one else will. But for me mastery is the greatest enemy. In an institutional setting one manifestation of this is the pressure to make things "work." (What we mean by "that works" of course is an endlessly variable and generally unexamined question which energizes me to jolt us all into a more mindful awareness of our own work, and you may notice me invoking a value in tension with this essay's "above all to stop thinking." But that is for some other think piece.) Rehearsal exists, in this case, to ensure that what we put on stage "works"; we triple check, we consult with outsiders and audiences, artistic directors invigilate the process energetically. Guaranteeing artistic quality is a crucial, perhaps the core, responsibility of their job. This of course leads us to value mastery. We want people in the theater who can reliably deliver a product with a consistent level of quality. So that is what we get: a stream of production that backflips away from any possibility of chaos, confusion or not-working. It is often highly competent, even very good, but that is just the problem. Its goodness (its quality in the strict sense) is of a kind we know in advance we will be comfortable with.

It seems to me that people talk about risk a great deal in nonprofit theater, and I am never quite sure what they mean. For me the thing worth risking artistically is that a choice or a gesture or an entire production really might fail. We have a hunch that something could be really exciting in a new way. Yes, a stern examination would probably reject such an impulse: That won't work! But what if we try and find out. What if we risk the possibility—no, the certainty—that some people in the audience won't respond favorably to the choice, in pursuit of the possibility of creating something truly surprising, new. In other words, it is an experiment, a calculated reasoned experiment, but one which nonetheless entails a higher degree of risk than our customary sense of control might admit. Even if the experiment we are testing fails spectacularly, we will enjoy a rare artistic adventure and enrich the culture with possibility. A special beauty of experiments is that when they fail, they succeed. When I say mastery is the enemy, one thing I mean is that I'd rather get an F than a C.

Yes, there are certain technical skills I have acquired, but they too easily become deadly habit. Yes, I sometimes feel the need to proclaim the legitimacy of my work (for funders, for the press, for TCG, for my ego), but sinking too much into that turn of mind leads to complacent self-regard. Yes, I am proud of my own work. But in my experience, no one made anything really important while they were thinking, "god, I'm good!" Maybe they thought that *and* some other things less pleasant. Restless dissatisfaction with self and its accompanying anguish make great things happen. So if I am thinking I can handle a theatrical challenge, I lose interest. I am driven to do things I do not know how to do and I strive to create situations precisely where *I do not know what's happening or going to happen.* Which brings us back to forced failure.

I am not saying that failure is the final goal. I do not want to get an F; I want an A. Failure as an integral stage of the creative process has an incomparable value. Directors in particular tend to favor control and articulation: They tell people what to do, and they are good at explaining. Although these are important skills, I am not wholly convinced that they lead to the most exciting work onstage; they guarantee the competent work I discuss above. Painters who have achieved a high level of technical excellence will speak of their desire to "break their hand." Brice Marden was driven to give up using brushes and paint with sticks; Francis Bacon used to throw paint at the canvas. So I strive to give up control. Forced failure is an important tool for this, but there are many others. The collaborative nature of theater and the severe material restrictions of the profession perpetually thwart our control. Unexpected or irrational events surprise me and force me to adjust my own approach to the work every hour. I embrace them. I also tend to resist explanation. If the production I create is wholly explicable in words, if directing means staging an account of a text that is translatable into language, then something very dear has been lost. That thing is my goal.

Of course I am lying. This whole embrace of randomness, chaos and failure, is built on my own strong sense of mastery. I do not mean that I am some great artistic master; I just mean I am competent to create a production and I know it. If we need to stage the play and tech it and open it by Wednesday, I can do it. If someone needs to be told what to do, or if they need an explanation, I can provide it. I just find it much more interesting to let go. And if failure is a stage of the process it bears fruit because I then subject the work to intense and sustained editing and shaping. I try to keep all the random failures in the mix, but only some of them actually survive the process in the final production. In the end the struggle between mastery and failure is where the action is. That tension creates a particular kind of awkward beauty. All those stutters and sputters create their own surprising music. Call it the poetry of the inarticulate. We confront odd and mysterious creations, what Hopkins calls "counter, original, spare, strange; whatever is fickle, freckled (who knows how?)" We don't know how! We may touch on deep truths and ineffable feelings in ways we could never explain. That at least is my hope and my belief.

David Herskovits is the Founding Artistic Director of Target Margin Theater in New York City, where he stages work from Shakespeare to Stein and devises new work based on existing sources. David has directed plays and operas at theaters, festivals and universities in the USA and abroad.

INNOVATION/COLLABORATION

Michael John Garcés

"The Shock of the New," right? The attempt, the desire, the struggle to make something new, in the hope that it will shock others, and even (especially?) ourselves, into response. Authentic, unmediated response. Experiencing art, and thus the world, in a different, exciting and possibly even revelatory way. An era of traumatic and thrilling technological innovation, certainly. The telegraph! The train! Mustard gas! Relativity! The zipper! Moving pictures! The production line! The airplane! The splitting of the atom! The satellite! TV! Napalm! The photocopier! Facebook! M-theory! YouTube! The way we live now changes and changes and changes, one is confronted daily, hourly by the new. And plays or performances are made in response. Animals react (and people do too, violently, or by breaking or shutting down), but humans respond. Theatre, creativity, as a necessary quality of the human. Yes? But a play written or performance created twenty, ten, three years ago is so full of archaisms and outdated references as to seem merely quaint. To seem other. The play you are writing now will lose relevance before it is finished. How to respond to *that*?

High art and low, commercial and non-, whatever the context, whatever the imagined dichotomy might be, artists strive to innovate, to introduce the new, to achieve impact. This impact is in and of itself value because it is so fucking hard to make impact living and working when everything is changing, everything is new and then new again, and the rate of that change increases geometrically. Our nostalgia horizon diminishes yearly. One thinks back to that innocent age twelve years ago, before 9/11 (seven years ago, before Twitter? Two years ago before Hurricane Sandy and the realization that global warming already happened? That misty, lost time before blogs and "Theater 2.0"?). Society in ten years (less? five?) will be unrecognizable, much less the world our children inhabit now, their brains *functioning* differently than ours in response to the world we have made for them. They currently live in a future we predict but will never actually know. Our innovations are obsolete even as they are made.

So, anxiety. Stress stress stress. How to make something new in the context of this form, theater or whatever, something in the context of a tired old unplugged and offline form that could possibly respond adequately, much less begin to live up to the tremendous engine of transformation that is contemporaneity?

Shakespeare, the great, inspiring and oppressively preponderant great-grandaddy of all English-language playmakers was nothing if not an innovator. In subject, in language, in responding to the paradigm-shattering innovations of recent centuries (the rate of change was slower, but the impact was perhaps greater as Europeans woke up slowly, in a bit of a daze, to the realization that the earth was round, royalty not divine, and they were floating insignificantly on the margins of a vast universe...). Shakespeare, the radical innovator, the incandescent writer (and not the dreary "bard of Avon"). So there is that to live up to. A tradition, and expectation, of making it new. Innovation is not, in and of itself, an innovation, of course—not new. In fact, it is quite traditional. Not so shocking.

So.

Innovation. The introduction of something new. Something that wasn't there until it was. Is. Something created. For better or worse. Innovations are not inherently, in and of themselves, good.

Of course, most innovations fail and pass unremarked. Wrong time, wrong place. Advantage isn't taken.

Something *truly* new would very likely be unrecognizable, and almost certainly unpremeditated.

So.

Innovation likely happens when there is, in the self, a real and committed willingness to change. To change perspective, to change beliefs and paradigms, to change in ways that are unanticipated. It takes discipline and commitment to be, and remain, open to change.

Innovation is fostered by collaboration. Ben Krywosz taught me that collaboration is what happens when two or more people interact to create a shared understanding that none previously possessed or could have achieved on their own.

I would go farther to say that, in true collaboration, the end result, whatever it be, is truly unknown. Sure, we may know we are making a play, we think we know what it's about, we know the text, even the style, perhaps (although we might not know any of those things!) but we really don't know what it's going to be until we do it, and are open to what happens when we are in process—that is, to me, collaboration. And that process carries the potential for innovation.

Something that theater, impoverished as it may or may not be, does, at its best, is create the possibility for a spectator to change. For that person to become, if only for a moment, new, to renew, to break through. This potential exists in virtually any performance, although it is rarely achieved. This potential exists regardless of form or content. It can, and does, happen by accident. The innovation might be a particular interaction in the gazillionth production of *The Glass Menagerie*, or the approach to a number in the crassest of jukebox musicals, or it might be the most delicately constructed nuance in the final masterpiece of an artist who has dedicated an entire life to a discipline of creativity. It is the incredibly potent energy within any production of any play.

Craft, rigor, discipline, dedication, intent, mission. The art is in achieving something approaching consistency in making this kind of breakthrough. So that it is not mere chance.

Innovation. We are confronted with a problem, and it is in the unexpectedness of the *nature* of what confronts us, of the specificity, even if we saw it coming, that prompts a response, and in that response is an innovation. We can do no more than create the conditions for creative response. By working hard at craft, by relaxing, by channeling passion, by collaborating.

Michael John Garcés is the artistic director of Cornerstone Theater Company, an ensemble with a practice centered in community-engaged art-making, in Los Angeles, and is a company member at Woolly Mammoth in Washington, D.C. He has worked as a director and writer at venues across the country and also frequently collaborates with performance artist Marc Bamuthi Joseph, having directed *the break/s* and *red, black and GREEN: a blues*, touring to venues such as BAM, The Walker and REDCAT.

DOING THE WORK

Rachel Jendrzejewski

It's 9pm. Truth be told, I am torn between wanting to surrender to watching a film with my partner and cats (the epitome of comfort) versus wanting to work on this post (pushing around words without knowing where they will take me, the labor and uncertainty and exhilaration of articulation). Both appealing options, but one is very cozy while the other requires going out on a limb, opening myself up. I've been noticing this negotiation between ritual and risk in every facet of my life lately—probably because it's a big theme in my ongoing collaboration with the Minneapolis-based contemporary performance ensemble SuperGroup (Jeff Wells, Sam Johnson and Erin Search-Wells).

Our work started years ago, before we knew each other well. I was living in Providence and collecting stories from acquaintances. I wanted to marry my years working collaboratively with communities through Cornerstone Theater Company with my time spent in Poland exploring language and the boundaries of form. I started interviewing people from the many different places in which I had lived, asking about their experiences in transit (literally, on trains, planes, buses, cars), with the intention of intertwining their stories into a play for bus lines. It was an exciting challenge; but when the time came to write, I couldn't find my way in. Everything I wrote felt phony.

I ditched the early drafts and poured back through the stories I had gathered. I realized I loved them because they encompassed not only experiences in transit but also transition—geographic, physical, professional, political and spiritual transition. Moments of epiphany, significant life change, if only recognized in retrospect. I decided to shelve my own writing for a while, but to continue collecting stories, now deliberately inviting anecdotes related to this broader idea of transition. Moments when people decided to make a big change, or found themselves facing a change beyond their control. The stories kept coming—specific, layered, nuanced.

In 2011, I moved to Minneapolis on a Playwrights' Center Jerome Fellowship. For a few months, I stayed with friends I had met through

Cornerstone. In the time since I'd last seen them, they had formed SuperGroup; and as I got to know their work, I realized we were on parallel paths of performative exploration. Thinking about dimensions of human experience besides event-driven narrative. Exploring sensory experience and bodily knowledge. Investigating the insufficiency of language. Examining how different ways of relating to "story" can complicate concepts like "identity," "community" and "culture." My fellowship included some development funds, typically used to pay a director and actors for readings, but I asked the Playwrights' Center if I could use those funds for preliminary explorations with SuperGroup instead. They said yes (one of many reasons I love the Playwrights' Center), and so we did just that. A collaboration was born.

I talked to SuperGroup about wanting to find a way into those transition stories. Movement suddenly made sense as the way forward. We decided I should write a very rough draft of text, SuperGroup would come up with movement structures based on the text, and then we'd layer them together and see what happened. I gave myself permission to not use the stories in an overt way, as I'd been doing before; instead I started looking at their layers and the collection as a whole. I started noticing themes and patterns. Rather than pointing to predictable milestones, for example (love at first sight, broken hearts, births, deaths, graduations), many of the transition stories focused on mundane moments. Fleeting conversations with strangers. Staring out windows. False alarms. I wrote a series of unordered meditations. Then SuperGroup and I holed up together at the Playwrights' Center. They generated structured improvisations and culled movement from the language. We learned some of the text and movement, then tried layering them together in different ways. We experimented. We played. We took breaks to talk about what was happening and what was coming up for us. We became acutely curious about the function that seemingly insignificant moments play in our lives. How, individually and collectively, little moments add up into big moments, accumulating into enormous rippling effects like love or climate change. We wondered, what might we learn by digging deeper into these patterns?

We spent about 14 months in development, meeting three times per week in the studio to explore and dig and make. We shared the culmination of that phase in a performance called *it's [all] highly personal*, presented as part of the Walker Art Center's Momentum:

New Dance Works 2013. All four of us appeared in the piece, and we recruited three additional cast members, plus invited the audience to participate in some pre-show activity before taking their seats. While I wrote the bulk of the text and SuperGroup steered the physicality, we all ultimately contributed to all aspects of the piece. We sewed our own costumes, brainstormed lighting desires to share with our designer and fundraised like mad. Both the process and what emerged from it were unlike anything I had made before—tessellations of text, sound and movement; strange happy accidents; unexpected emotion. It was extremely gratifying to watch the work cohere into its own distinct, visceral, alive self. Shortly following the close of the production, we resumed our studio practice to advance and expand our explorations together.

Now, I won't attempt to judge whether our work is "innovative" in the grand scheme of performance history; but I am contemplating the fact that this buzzword, "innovation," ultimately just means doing the work that artists have always done. It's a pretty modest ancient concept; *Merriam-Webster*'s definition reads, "to make changes: do something in a new way." That's it. Ask questions. Pursue answers. Explore, risk, make something new. Or make something old in a new way. Sometimes I think we've put "innovation" on a pedestal, reserving it for luminaries like Steve Jobs, when in fact, at heart, it's pretty basic. Just do the work of making theater. The results might be radical—a new kind of play that goes down in history!—or they might be subtle. I think of those seemingly mundane moments that stuck with my interviewees as most significant in retrospect. Innovation can be as simple as taking a different route to rehearsal today, so that you enter the space with new images in your brain. Of course, who knows where that experience, combined with a thousand more like it, will lead? Quite possibly, we will make new kinds of plays that go down in history after all.

I know it's easier said than done. It can be downright terrifying to take artistic risks, knowing that they might not be acknowledged or appreciated in this lifetime, let alone cover the rent. It also can be really frightening to walk down a new street, not knowing if it will be welcoming. Particularly in this funding landscape, it can be very difficult and lonely to trust that the effort of "doing the work" is worthwhile, even if the impact isn't immediately obvious or easily quantified.

So then, some questions for all of us—if artistic innovation is a priority in this field (and buzz indicates that it is), how might theatres keep evolving to facilitate "doing the work" of it? How might freelance artists support each other better? And how might these parties interact more meaningfully and equitably toward sharing practices, knowledge and resources? It's never absolute, but I know many artists who would benefit from more stability, and many organizations that could earnestly enjoy some disruption. I could talk about how I want to revolutionize the whole system. Yet I also keep thinking of that fundamental tension between security and risk. My guess is that, no matter what happens, we all have to keep stretching.

If we practice being open—really, truly, proactively open—to small "innovations" in our daily lives, disciplines and relationships, might not those efforts accumulate into more comprehensive field-wide innovation? I'm not just talking about new plays, of course, but new play-making processes. Not just "ensemble-devised work," but artists and institutions working together in all kinds of configurations we can't even imagine yet. Not just splashy, marketable innovation, but also (and more importantly) small-yet-mighty shifts in habit and perspective, individually and collectively.

The question becomes—what is your work today?

Rachel Jendrzejewski is a playwright and performance-maker. Her work has been produced by the Walker Art Center, Red Eye Theater and Padua Playwrights, among others. Honors include a Playwrights' Center Jerome Fellowship and numerous grants. She holds an MFA in Playwriting from Brown University. *www.rachelka.com*

YAY, INNOVATION! WAIT, INNOVATION?

Chris Wells

When asked to write about Innovation in the Theatre, I thought, *Yay! Innovation.* I love innovation. This was followed almost immediately by some less-than-sexy thoughts—*Wait, Innovation? What is innovation?* Here are some thoughts and questions that remain following the showdown between *Yay, Innovation!* and *Wait, Innovation?*

IT'S PERSONAL. How may I push myself to make work that is responding to the ever-changing world around and within me? It's easy to find that thing you're good at and then just do it for the rest of your life with little change. For inspiration, I look to folks like Joni Mitchell and Bjork, the Canadian dance company La La La Human Steps, the collection of the American Visionary Art Museum in Baltimore; artists who continually push/ed themselves to break open again and again to find new ways of expressing what must come out.

RISK. I've been a performer for over 30 years, a writer for 15 and a producer for 10, and the thing that makes me most excited is risk; it's become a benchmark for me—if it doesn't have risk in it, it's not art. This is what it means to be a shaman, right? To be willing to step into the circle, to take on the feelings, stories and values of the entire village and, just before beginning the rite to think, "Well, this might have been a really bad idea, but I'm here to be transformed, right? So, here we go..."

LET'S RESPOND TO OUR FEELINGS! Seven years ago, after doing a bunch of regional theatre, it dawned on me that I was being hired to entertain rich people between dinner and bedtime. The work I was taking part in was confirming a limited worldview. That realization hit me in the early part of the run, so every night it sunk in deeper that my values didn't matter, my perceptions didn't matter, in short, that *I* didn't matter. After the show closed, I took a break from acting to get back in touch with what I wanted to say.

COMMUNITY. In 2007, I started the Secret City, a performance ritual that combines the structure of a religious service with artistic content as a means to explore the sacred in art. I wanted the spirit back in my theatre, and the theatre back in my spirit. And I don't mean god, but spirit—the essence that connects us all and that is most easily found in art. The Secret City meets monthly in New York City and quarterly in LA. In the next several years, we'll be expanding to cities around the country and the world. Community-building and connection-seeking is innovative.

MORE ART THAT LEADS TO RIOTING. The other day was the 100th anniversary of the premiere of Stravinsky's *Rite of Spring* in Paris. I was working on a blog posting about it, so was reading up on that amazing event a century ago. The music Stravinsky wrote was radical, for sure, but on top of that, Nijinsky had choreographed the piece in a style that is controversial even today. The most telling anecdote from that night was this: At one point, Nijinsky stood in the wings, stomping out the rhythm on the stage floor, because the dancers could not hear the orchestra over the screaming of the enraged audience.

IT'S EASY TO CRITICIZE. I used to dine out on my ability to tear apart somebody else's work, and thrill to the delicious taste of righteous anger. I still feel the pull to be negative, to take personally every experience that doesn't please me. In the past several years, I've become far more appreciative of anyone who accomplishes anything in this world; seriously—it is so hard to get anything done! Creating anything is innovative. Nowadays, I actively attempt to be more compassionate, more understanding, more encouraging.

LEADERSHIP ISN'T JUST FOR LEADERS ANYMORE. You can be a leader by making work that you care about, living where you feel you can make a difference, interacting with your community in ways that might be unexpected. A lot of us feel that we're powerless to impact the world, but at every level of society, in every department of an organization, in any role of a family, we have the power to make choices that impact ourselves and our institutions.

WHO ELSE IS HERE? Perhaps I'm codependent, but I'm not just interested in the show on the stage, but the show in the house, too. Over the years, I've done a lot of cabaret work, and I love that dangerous, live connection one feels in a great cabaret experience. In making theatre, I want to touch the people I'm speaking to—not just entertain them, or provide an experience for them to consume, or vote thumbs up/ thumbs down, but to actually say, "We are all in the room together, having a real, live, shared experience." And, I want the presence of those people to inform the theatre being made.

COMMUNICATION. All the world's problems could be improved by more intentional communication. We see that in our personal and professional relationships. And, artists are the keepers of communication, the ones charged with expressing the difficult, beautiful, dark, substantive truths about being alive. So, how do we use the tools we have to impact the world around us?

COLLABORATION. It's hard to resist the pull toward hierarchical structures and the thrill of power. Collaboration asks us to acknowledge our shared humanity, and to rise above our ego-driven agendas. It's also helpful to seek out other art forms. One of my favorite parts of making theatre is the first day of rehearsal when the dramaturg brings in pictures of dance, or film clips, or a story from a faraway place explaining how seemingly disparate things inform each other. Expansion is innovative.

SINCERITY. Sincerity is not the same as boring. Sincerity means that you mean what you say. The saddest thing is to sit through something that leaves one feeling like life doesn't matter and that leaving the house was a waste of time. All we have are our choices—to apply sincerity to our choices is key. This is mindfulness in art, to mean what we say and do, and to believe that these choices make a difference in the world. Bitterness is not innovative.

INVENTION IS NOT INNOVATION. For an art form that has been left in the dust by recent inventions—TV, radio, film, the internet—it's important to look at what is inherent in live performance and to lean into it. Now more than ever, we need the live event to remind us that we rely on each other. We need to be able to sit in a room together and experience an exchange of feelings, thoughts, joy and silence.

EXCLUSIVITY. There are a lot of people who like to limit access to power. It's probably related to living in a capitalistic culture, but we are corrupted with the idea that, while there may be enough for everybody, not necessarily everybody should have it. So, generosity is innovative, sharing is innovative, telling someone about a great opportunity that you might be up for yourself, is innovative. And, trust; that there is more than enough for everyone and that you can let go of control—that's innovative.

SHAKESPEARE IS NOT INNOVATIVE. Seriously, people put on a lot of Shakespeare. And he's amazing, right? I know, that sounds lame but, I get it. A lot of really talented people feel passionately about his work and do it beautifully. So, this might just be me looking for a fight, but can we take a break? Can we have a national moratorium on producing Shakespeare in any shape or form for, I don't know, five years? We're not getting rid of him, we're saying, Hey, Shakespeare, you're amazing, and we're so grateful for what you've done for the theatre, the world, humanity. We love you SO much!! Now, here's a ticket to Tahiti, and a nice cottage on the beach with catered meals. Maybe take up painting for a while? Meanwhile, back home, let's look for people whose voices we've not heard enough, or never heard at all, and let's produce their work! Imagine what's out there, being made out of bottle caps and grass, song fragments and found letters, anger and frustration, archeological finds and fresh dreaming. Let's champion those people! Let's make work that threatens us, pushes us out of our comfort zone, wakes us up, forces us to meet each other and leads to riots. In a few years, when Shakespeare comes back from Tahiti and we take him to see a show he might say, "Wow, I've never seen anything like this. This is fantastic stuff. I mean, really fantastic. I wish I'd thought of that."

Chris Wells is an Obie Award–winning actor, writer, teacher and community leader. In 2007, he created the Secret City–part salon, part ceremony, part tent revival. *www.thesecretcity.org*. He lives in Woodstock where he is completing his first book, *The Bermuda Triangle Inn–a memoir in 29 stories. www.mrchriswells.com*

VERNACULAR THEATRE
AND THE GREAT FEAST

Catherine Love

Within the theatre community, it's become common to hear about the turn toward participation. Increasingly, works of contemporary art and theatre are being made *with* audiences as well as *for* them, recruiting participants to actively shape the final artistic material. Here the process is just as important as the product—indeed, for those who take part, it might be more important than what they eventually produce.

London Bubble's *From Docks to Desktops*, which I followed throughout some of its development, is one such example. The show was collaboratively created by its participants, who gathered experiences of working life from their local communities in South East London over a number of months. London Bubble's home in Rotherhithe is at the heart of an area of the city that has seen some of the most dramatic changes to both its landscape and its structures of employment in the last few decades; where once thrived docks and factories is now the home of lucrative property developments and shopping centers. The show that the company stitched together from the collected material reflected the socio-economic shifts in this specific area of London and its impact on the people living there.

Crucially, the process of *From Docks to Desktops* was inscribed in its performance. It was performed by the same participants who helped to gather the material that formed the piece and it was framed by the act of interviewing. This offered audiences a route into the stories being told, while at the same time allowing an appreciation of the work simultaneously on the levels of process and product. It also built in space for the encounter with its audiences—many of whom, of course, were from the area it is concerned with, and some of whose stories contributed to its creation.

Director Jonathan Petherbridge has a particular language for discussing London Bubble's intergenerational work and it's a helpful one to adopt. In explaining the process of collecting and curating stories from the local community, he uses the vocabulary of food: Ingredients are foraged through a long process of interviews and the findings are prepped by workshop groups before being passed over to professional artists to create a recipe, which will then in turn be tasted and tweaked by everyone involved. It all ends, of course, in a great feast. While this is neat as an analogy, it's also particularly apt. Preparing and eating a meal together involves an unspoken act of community, one that is also heavily present in this kind of work.

Since *From Docks to Desktops* came to an end, London Bubble has been asking where its foraging might take it next. The company is currently working with participants on *Hopelessly De-Voted*, a project examining the local community's relationship—both good and bad—with Britain's electoral system ahead of the 2015 general election. It's the first time that the company's particular methodology has been applied to a contemporary topic, with the potential for cooking up a feast with an altogether different flavor.

Through the journey it takes on its way to the stage, London Bubble's intergenerational work forms a community that crosses barriers of age and artistic practice at the same time as embedding itself firmly within an often neglected sense of place. Petherbridge has coined the term "vernacular theatre" to describe this work; like vernacular architecture, it is "hewn from local material and shaped by local knowledge." It serves a specific use for a specific community, and its very material is drawn from within that community. It is, essentially, a community discovering and telling its own stories. And in a political context in which we are implicitly told that community no longer exists and our stories are not worth telling, this feels like an increasingly radical act.

Catherine Love is a freelance theatre critic and arts journalist whose work has appeared in publications including the *Guardian, The Stage, Time Out* and *Exeunt*. Since graduating with a degree in English from the University of Southampton in 2011, she has also worked as an administrator, researcher and copywriter.

TWO LAUNCH PADS

Pedro de Senna

So, what's new? I really mean it. If we are talking about Artistic Innovation (yes, with capitals), we need to define our terms. And what's artistic? Does Artistic Innovation equate to what's new in art? Philosopher Morris Weitz has claimed that attempting to define art would necessarily restrict the inherent creativity involved in its coming into being—it would certainly restrict its newness, which gives me the impression that true art is always innovative (though not all innovation is artistic). So perhaps the question to be asked is not *what* is new or innovative in art, but *for whom*?

When I was little I remember learning about Columbus and his 1492 "discovery" of the Novo Mundo, the New World. Though what came to be known as the American continent had been around for quite a while (geologists assure me, though creationists might dispute it) and had been home to millions of people by the time the intrepid Genovese arrived on a Spanish ship, it was still treated as "new" by European (and Eurocentric) historiographers and geographers until well into the late twentieth century, in an attitude that was reflected in my own primary-school education in Brazil. And what to say of Oceania, the *Novíssimo Mundo*? Newness indeed.

Why write about history and geography? Avant-garde artists at the turn of the twentieth century looked for the new not only in the old, but also on the foreign: Yeats and his Noh plays, Artaud and his Balinese theatre are just two of a number of innovators for whom the encounter with traditions alien to them and to their audiences caused the shock of the new. Contemporary Western theatre makers, from Brook to Mnouchkine to McBurney still do it. As Caridad pointed out, "[i]t's all about the moment. The moment of contact." Newness does not come into being in and of itself. It happens between agents. So for the new to happen in art, artists need to meet. In conferences, virtual or real, and in festivals, but also and importantly in universities and in that in-between space created by translation.

I'd like to pay attention to these last two—I am after all, a lecturer and translator. These roles are uniquely privileged. As mediator between cultures and languages the translator is always bringing something new into existence. To stay with playwriting: Plays reach new audiences or, switching the perspective, audiences see new (to them) plays. Artists from one country are able to read and watch plays from another. Dramaturgical forms and practices are shared and disseminated. More, the translator straddles two linguistic worlds, where semantic fields don't overlap, and words do not necessarily correspond with one another. She needs to create neologisms, invent new ways of saying, expanding the realm of what is known and knowable within a language, allowing for discovery. Translation allows for an encounter with otherness, with an Other displaced geographically and historically. Thanks to translation, we understand more about ourselves, and in our ability to read and watch Chekhov, Aristophanes or Fermín Cabal (I am randomly looking at my bookshelf) we find inspiration for our own creativity. But again, it is not only the viewer/reader who is enlightened. The play itself becomes new, seen and read in new contexts, written afresh and reinscribed in a new culture. Translation is not only a bridge, it is a launchpad for innovation.

The other launchpad is of course education. Universities have been under sustained attack from policy-makers, both in the U.K. and in the U.S., with the closure of departments and the casualization/ adjunctification of academic staff in both countries being symptoms of a market-led conception of education. These symptoms, however, are also potentially the cause of an important loss. Relations between faculties in different departments, conversations over coffee, time spent in the office talking to students, engaging as human beings, present, in dialogue, are lost when departments are shut and staff are not in permanent employment.

Twenty-five hundred years ago, Socrates already knew that learning happens best in conversation. Universities are uniquely set up as permanent fora where such conversations might happen. Theatre-makers with engineers, linguists with computer scientists, tutors with students. Yes, that moment of contact again. Because it is not only high-end, funder-friendly interdisciplinary research: Teaching within your discipline is also creating the new—and not only for the student. I cannot count the amount of times I have seen or read extracts from or essays about *Waiting for Godot*. Every time I talk about it with a student, or watch even a small section being performed by first-year undergraduates, I learn something–about me, about theatre, about the world. Something new comes into being.

Universities are spaces where this happens every day, and artists would do well to engage with them. There is a critical mass of young artists (i.e. students, future and present innovators) meeting and producing work, watching and responding to it, encountering and creating the new. It provides inspiration in many ways: showing students' work-in-progress, testing out ideas, discussing them in a safe forum, where experimentation and critical questioning is part of the job. Conversely, more universities should invite artistic residencies, if they are to become leaders in innovation, even in a market-oriented sector. Conversations and encounters, generating "unintended learning outcomes," to use the jargon of Edu speak. In other words, the new.

So support your universities, campaign for them, engage with them. And read a foreign play or two. This is where the new is at.

Pedro de Senna is a theatre practitioner and academic. He was born in Rio de Janeiro, where he started performing in 1993. He is a Senior Lecturer in Contemporary Theatre at Middlesex University and his research focuses on translation and adaptation, the relationship between directing and dramaturgy, and disability studies.

THE ACT OF INTRODUCING
SOMETHING NEW

Kali Quinn

How are we teaching the next generation of theatre artists to empower themselves as responsible, well-rounded creators? What has theatre education become if not to be The Place for reconnecting young people with their innate ability to play? To create. To be able to turn things into other things. To wonder more often. To be curious. To listen. To reimagine our world. To ask "what if?" and "why not?" A laboratory that relentlessly invests in the expansion of a point of view alongside the commitment to humbly and boldly sharing this evolving voice publically with others.

From audition to audience, realizing our own assumptions as theatre academics and practitioners is absolutely necessary for the development of innovative artistry. Instead of teaching what theatre is, an ensemble-based devised process of making theatre from the ground up invites us all to reenvision what theatre could be and how it can be made. What a better way to explore than with the raw, unfettered ideas of enthusiastic young practitioners who are hungry to learn and reinvent! If only we can let go of our own assumptions, follow the momentum of the ensemble and let them teach us, the product can become a group-owned performance rooted in the heart of play and collaboration: a distinct encounter that breeds contagious empowerment along with a future practice and reminder that teaching, making and delivering theatre is as an act of possibility and freedom, and in turn one of great responsibility and care.[10]

This article offers you potential methods for and inspirational glimpses into ensemble-based devised processes, with references to productions that I facilitated at Mississippi University for Women (2011), Brown University/Trinity Repertory MFA Program (2012)

---

[10] I have written 111 values for this kind of "Compassionate Creativity" which can be found at: *www.compassionatecreativity.com*

and Bucknell University (2013).[11] As you draw from my experiences below, let me also connect you to the giants whose shoulders I stand upon, reminding you of your own lineage of dedicated theatre makers. I am privileged and grateful to extend my teachers' points of view by continuing to introduce new students to the infinite possibilities of play.

PART 1: THE SPARK

PROPOSING SOMETHING THAT DOESN'T YET EXIST

"We don't know where we're going exactly, but we're sure on our way there!"

—Elaine Williams
Scenographer & Professor of Theatre & Dance
Bucknell University

As a facilitator in the devised process, I am constantly learning about and balancing each ensemble member's sense of discomfort with the unknown. It is of utmost importance that I gain their trust, in order to lead them through this uncharted territory in a way that allows for them to remain open, listening, and enthusiastic.

So I admit and remain transparent about our starting point: At the beginning of this devised process we stand looking out off the edge of an abyss. A dark, wide-open void of the unknown. Scary, risky AND the perfect place for creativity and innovation, if only we don't run away screaming into the night overwhelmed by the possibilities. So we need some limitations. Some checkpoints. Both artistic and logistic. What do we already know? These "limitations" become light posts in the darkness that we gather around and in order to begin our play. These lights will slowly broaden illuminating islands of information. Islands that can ground us when all might seem lost. These islands might be themes. They might be interests. They include the skills or challenges of the group. If we can hold faith that these islands of knowns are

---

[11] Production blogs that documented each process can be found at:
www.kaliquinn.com

somehow connected under water, they will soon begin to migrate toward one another as our process unfolds. We cannot waste precious time worrying about what it will be. We can simply invest, one flicker at a time, in how it can be by playing it out.

KEEPING A FINGER ON THE PULSE OF THE ENSEMBLE

"When you don't know what to do, stop doing. Hold still, breathe and listen. Keep listening. Listen to everything, and especially listen to anything that keeps coming up."
—Sally Goers Fox
Retired Voice & Movement Teacher
University of Rochester & University of Buffalo

At first we will all wear every hat. Yes. We will think, sometimes simultaneously, as playwrights, performers, designers, directors, characters and observers. Now please don't get me wrong, I love specializations in the theatre, but sometimes believe this happens way too soon. An actor is never just an actor but rather a creative being that needs to be able to see from every perspective in order to best play his or her part in the whole. Eventually as the process goes on, I will begin to zoom out further into the role of director and the students will zoom in further as actors expressing themselves as characters that they created themselves. Going from a more of a horizontal or consensus-based way of working to more vertical or hierarchical way of working can feel abrupt and cause tension, so it is imperative to articulate when and how this shift happens.

In every phase of the process, I've learned better how not to force my ideas, but rather to listen to what is already happening and, even more importantly, to admit when I don't have the answer. Not in an emotional, apologetic or declaiming way, but rather as fact. A shrug of the shoulders. An arms wide open for new ideas. A listening breath at the crossroads. When I am in this moment, I look to the ensemble: "I'm not sure what to do now. I need three options of what to do next. Anybody, anybody?" And then I choose to explore one of those in order to move us all forward.

PART 2: THE PROCESS

MOVING TOGETHER FIRST

"What is true in the physical world is probably also true in the metaphysical world and vice versa. As an actor, your role is to act, not wait. You are a creator. You don't have to wait for the part, create it. Things that are in motion tend to stay in motion and things that are at rest tend to stay at rest. This simply means that when you wake up every morning either you go to work on a role that has been offered to you, or you create a role of your own devising."

—Daniel Stein
Head of Movement & Physical Theatre
Brown University/Trinity Rep

I prefer getting to know people at first by moving with them. An EXERCISE to begin with: "Please take a moment to balance out our space with our bodies. Now everyone inhale while raising one foot. Keep the idea of the inhale going. See the possibility, anticipation, and the who-knows-what-we-might-make-together, under your foot. Inhale it all. Raise your eyebrows (this will always help everything). On the exhale, we will take our first step into this project today. Ready? Go..."

INHABITING SUSPENSION

"When disaster strikes and the normal person might panic, the clown surveys the situation and says to herself, "Interesting." This detente—physical, psychological and emotional—allows time and space for the audience to join the clown in imagining multiple creative solutions to the problem."

—Avner "the Eccentric" Eisenberg
Clown, Performer, Director & Educator

"...Now freeze." We tend to do this when we experience what I like to call an "Oh Shit" moment: moments where you don't know what to do. Can someone give me an example of an "Oh Shit" moment you had in the last twenty-four hours:

"I locked myself out the house."

"My alarm didn't go off."

"Finding out that my in-laws house burned down."

When we hear these moments it automatically begins to change the way we breathe. Interesting. Our body is ready to react. To engage. To empathize. Intrigued by what someone might do next. How they might deal with this situation. "Oh Shit" moments are interesting territory that we enjoy watching someone else navigate, and boy do we learn an immense amount about ourselves, each other and our characters in these moments of uncertainty. Not necessarily by *what* people do, but by *how* they react.

Now, inevitably, in these moments we freeze, seeing these moments as an interruption rather than part of what's happening. We freeze finding ourselves somewhere that we had not planned to be. We want to be somewhere else. Anywhere else. We want to shut down, implode, hold our breath and become skeptical, quickly moving onto the next thing we know to do. But "you aren't stuck in traffic, you are the traffic."[12]

Our creation process will be full of "Oh Shit" moments. And you can freeze up, shut down and give up or you can truly breathe into your own "Oh Shit" moment (or someone else's) and discover a kind of suspension in the not knowing. A different experience of time that begs us to be present, one where we begin to create space, express ourselves, discover connections, see opportunities and excitedly ask questions that don't necessarily have answers. These moments suddenly become reminders to wake up and reconnect with our sense of creativity and compassion. To listen and connect to the other. To wonder. To reach out, letting our curiosity take us for a ride.

---

[12] I saw this saying on a billboard south of Boston in 2012.

"Be careful when you use the word 'weird.' It is a space-filler while attempting to talk about something that you do not understand. Something you do yet have the capacity to turn into words. Careful with that word."

—Adrian Mejia
Physical Performer & Classmate
Dell'Arte International

In creating new work, it's easy for ideas and moments to get lost in the ether. We must title and document new vocabulary so that we can refer to it as a common point of reference. Some ideas and tools discovered within these processes:

- **"This Reminds Me Of..."**—A way to connect what we are doing to other experiences or real-life experiences, along with other moments in the play.

- **Encourage Dynamic Rather Than Detail**—Starting to simplify and use bigger brushstrokes within our story where we focus on the dynamic or push and pull between two characters rather than a he said/she said way of thinking.

- **Stepping One Month at a Time**—Thinking and moving in a way where every step is one month or even one year in order to move in suspended time and at a higher physical volume with one direct intention.

- **Think with Your Hands**—Showing us just what you are thinking, feeling, being affected by, just by isolating your movement to your hands. Try with other parts of the body.

- **Metaphor Wash**—How could what that person just said or did be thought of as more of a symbol or metaphor that relates to another part of our story?

- **Somebody Else**—Talking with someone outside of our process about what our play/process is like, what they think about it, and then bringing that conversation back to the ensemble.

> *"Things happen in the process of creative play, left/right brain
> connections that weren't there before, improved learning
> capacity in children and adults, renewals of agency, and that
> is just the beginning of the list. These things are, at the very
> least, grist for new thinking about what art is and how we
> can use it in our lives, and they ought to be reason enough to
> restructure our educational system."*
> —Jo Carson in *Spider Speculations*
> Writer, Storyteller, Playwright, Founder of Alternate ROOTS

There are times in a devised process when we are out being hunters
and gatherers of new ideas to put in our pot. I think of this divergence
as an outward, opened-arm kind of energy. We are ready, creating and
accumulating new material. Then conversely there are times when we
are bringing all of these ideas together. I think of this convergence as a
funneling, creating a pathway to bring our discoveries into view: seeing
patterns, collaging ideas. Sometimes this second phase feels more
challenging as it begs for more decisions and letting go. Leaving some
things behind. We wax and wane between these two phases in order to
put our play into The Play:

Divergence (Characters): We start our process with physical play,
vocabulary building and possibly mask technique to help build
character. We then develop and inhabit characters from shape to
breath to movement to gesture to sound to text. Individual image
boards help the design team to get a feel for the direction we have
started off in. Little by little, through facilitated play, we start to learn
about the characters' loves, hates, hopes, fears, what they are good at
and what they find funny.[13]

Convergence (Relationships): Through character interviews along
with physical improvisation and play, we observe how the characters
relate to one another, start to form groups and take on status. Each

---

[13] This list comes from a set of *Prompts for Character Creation* that can be found at:
www.kaliquinn.com.

actor makes a family tree. At Bucknell the characters formed the following groups, informing costumes and a certain social structure amidst the characters: The Forgotton, The Builders, The Jackets and The Demons.[14]

Divergence (World): By recognizing certain patterns, themes and moments of heightened tension, we start to discover and play in the world that that these characters inhabit. Identifying "versus" or polarities or spectrums within the world also allows the group to find the rules of the world and its possible conventions begin to unfold. For example, at Brown/Trinity we explored reality versus fantasy and community versus the individual.

Convergence (Story): We title moments of interaction (lazzo) and start to see whether they feel like beginnings, middles or endings. A structure begins to emerge. We researched other stories that had that same structure. We then "lock in" or hinge story elements onto this structure. Things that can't change. Things agreed upon by the whole group stay and others are tabled until the next rehearsal. In Mississippi the woman playing the Queen hurt herself and was in a wheelchair for a week. Even though she healed, we decided to lock in the wheelchair.

And then, of course, the most challenging part: How do we end our play? The story? Our relationship with our audience? The inclination usually thrusts toward creating a story about good and bad or right and wrong. But the world doesn't need more of these kinds of stories. What if instead we echo our process and work to find an ending that is somehow about inclusion, one that goes deeper into the complexities of multiple points of view. That levitates questions without needing answers.

In Mississippi, for example, it was less than a week before opening and we couldn't figure how to end the piece. The play dealt with a two mystical witch sisters. One decided to seek out horrific revenge on the other by using her powers to have the baby of her sister's husband. Everyone wanted to punish the one sister. She seemed "evil." But it

---

[14] The costumes for this production were then designed by Paula D. Davis, Professor of Theatre & Dance at Bucknell University.

wasn't that easy. Sure, we could have killed her off and let the rest live happily ever after, but that wasn't what our process had been like. This would have felt like a complete turn away from everything we had been discovering as we created. Finally the night before we opened, doing several improvisations between the characters, we realized that the play was really about forgiveness. And if the audience left asking how one sister could possibly find it in herself to forgive the other, then that was a great place to send the audience off into the night.

PART 3: THE SHARING

EMPOWERING THE AUDIENCE

"The most unique aspect of our work is that the primary decision-making power rests in the hands of the artists. Ensemble theater is the antithesis of the corporate model that dominates the theatrical landscape in America today... Our work is committed to the unique event of the living stage, where the imagination of artist and audience is linked in social communion and mutual creativity."
　—Manifesto of the Network of Ensemble Theaters (NET)[15]

The program note at Bucknell read: "The characters, world and story you are about to witness was developed through improvisation, physical play and storytelling exercises. When interviewing students, faculty and community members about their relationship to power, one of our ensemble members, Emily Mack, brought quotes from medical professionals she worked with in Nicaragua. These statements shifted our perspective and the direction of our process: "Power is the ability to be loved. The more you're loved the more powerful you are. People that can engender love and are loved by others are powerful. If a person is loved and respected, they have more power and influence over others. Humans are connected by love. Power is the state of having and giving what you have to others." Everything you see and

---

[15] The full manifesto for the Network of Ensemble Theaters can be found at: *www.ensembletheaters.net*

hear today was created by this group of people in order to share it with you today. There is no "right way" to interpret this work. Enjoy choosing your own adventure."

After each show, the second act was with the audience—a conversation that I facilitated to hear how the audience was responding to what they had just witnessed. What were they thinking, feeling or wanting to do? What hooked them? What line did they follow? What was the ultimate sinker? Ultimately, what was their interpretation and how could we empower it further?

The ensemble sits back and listens as the audience articulated moments from their adventures back to us for over a half hour: "The fabric becoming a baby, the sisters fighting, time passing...transformation, forgiveness, community reconciliation...How in the heck did you all make this?"

STICKING A STAKE INTO THE GROUND

"Drive a stake in the ground of your being. It will mark your faith, your belief and your sacrifices, so that if/when you slip, you will have something to grab hold of. And by holding on you can declare, 'This is my path.' And then standing you can say, 'And this is what I love.'"
—Ronlin Forman on Point of View
School Director, Dell'Arte International

When I devise a piece of theatre with a group of people, I feel like we are changing the world. How? By operating under a different way of working that is "un-systemetizable." Instead of saying, "Here is your part or role and this is how you are expected to fill it," we are saying, "Who are you? What can you bring? What do you want to say?" This can be a huge paradigm shift for students and professionals (in all fields). A flip of the coin. The act of introducing something new. Instead of telling someone what to do, we are giving them permission to allow themselves to do. To create. To be. There is no audition. Anyone who wants to be in that room can be in that room. Day after day we each actively choose to show up and participate. Invest. There is no cast in this devised piece. Little by little we create an ensemble. I do not tell that ensemble who they are or even how to talk with one another. What drives the group to become an ensemble is each individual's level of involvement, and how each individual articulates herself or himself within the process. At the first rehearsal we make a set of agreements on ways to work. We create a common language through physical play, by titling our discoveries so that they can become tools with which we create. A way of communicating with one another about what we want to have happen again. And how. To remember something that might have excited us. A group memory. We make observations. We witness one another. It is the responsibility as the facilitator of a devised process to cultivate ways of ensuring that everyone can be heard. An act of introducing someone to their own voice. To nurture that voice. To find various ways for everyone to be present and at their best. Their essence. To acknowledge one another. And to consistently encourage a space for people to listen to each other, even and especially when there may be disagreements. To navigate these moments peacefully and productively. To discover ways to move forward without forcing an outcome. To establish group ritual by recognizing the repetition. The patterns. The tendencies. To have your finger on the pulse of the moment. To allow the work and play to teach us what wants to happen next. To always remember to start exactly where we are. To meet each another there: a breeding ground for innovation, creativity, transformation and imagination. To invite an audience in and wholeheartedly share these discoveries and possibilities with them. This process, my friends and colleagues, reflects the kind of world I strive to live in.

Kali Quinn has performed solo work, directed, or designed movement at Ko Festival, Duke University, HERE Arts Center, Pearl Theatre Company, Bloomsburg Theatre Ensemble, Celebration Barn, MIT, Clowns Without Borders, Grupo Galpao/Brazil and Accademia Dell'Arte/Italy. Kali served on the Board of the Network of Ensemble Theaters, graduated from University of Rochester and Dell'Arte International, and now teaches at Brown University.

'TIS NEW TO THEE

Mark Schultz

If we're going to talk about innovation, I think there might be worse places to start than with acknowledging this: Innovation has nothing to do with being new.

So. Okay. What does that mean?

One of my favorite bits of Shakespeare is that moment in *The Tempest* when Miranda marvels wide-eyed at the glorious assembly of wealthy and powerful men that has suddenly appeared in the middle of her chess match with Ferdinand. Unable to control herself, she exclaims, "O, wonder!/How many goodly creatures are there here!/How beauteous mankind is! O brave new world,/That has such people in't!" It's a nice moment.

It's nice, mostly, because we want to believe her. But we can't. Because (as Jan Kott points out in his essay "Prospero's Staff"), unlike Miranda, we know what this assembly is. We've seen these people in action: traitors, criminals, their handlers and enablers. Miranda's hopefulness is so beautiful, but so delicate—a little knowledge spoils it completely. Prospero's response acknowledges the deep irony of the situation with such great and real tenderness: " 'Tis new to thee," he says, and we can almost hear his heart breaking as he says it.

"'Tis new to thee."

This moment says something very true about the nature of newness. And it's not so much that the new will eventually get old—everything gets old. That's life. We all know that. No, I think this moment in *The Tempest* speaks to the complexity of newness by creating a lovely human tension between Miranda and Prospero, innocence and experience. This tension shows us, first, that newness is a subjective, not an absolute value. It is fleeting. Easily dissipated. Ephemeral and evanescent. After our experience of the new, the moment's gone. It's not new anymore. And chances are very very good that it was only ever new to us, and that for but a moment. But, second, it shows us that newness, as fleeting as it is, represents something to which it's important to remain connected. The new isn't a thing, an object, it's an *experience*. Moreover, it's an experience of wonder: an acknowledgement that we don't completely know everything that the human adventure has in store for us, even though that adventure is only new to us.

Prospero, paraphrasing the Teacher in Ecclesiastes, tells us there is nothing new under the sun. And he's right. Miranda shows us that newness is an experience of the world and a disposition to the world that looks like wonder. And she's right, too.

But it gets complicated. Because we can talk about Prospero and Miranda and newness-as-wonder-while-acknowledging-that-nothing-is-new all we want, but we live in a particular time and place and are in a very deep relationship with the culture and values of our time and place. We live in a commercial culture that eschews Prospero's wisdom and can't comprehend Miranda's wonder beyond wanting to figure out how to package it and sell it. It's a culture where newness is only ever really about novelty—new stuff. New stuff is saleable stuff. Everybody wants new stuff. Everyone's going to want to buy new stuff. "New and improved" is a commercial trope that speaks volumes to what newness actually means to us: improvement. Better lives through the purchase of more new stuff. Of course we look at that trope—New and Improved—and we know it has more to do with marketing—with the manipulation of appearances, with a perception of something which may or may not be there—than it does with a sense of wonder at the really real. Still. Stuff that's new is appealing, even if it's only new in a theoretical or rhetorical sense.

We are so steeped in all of this theoretical/rhetorical newness that, more often than not, when we think about innovation, we tend to think that it means: making a new thing or saying a new thing. And we need Prospero and the Teacher of Ecclesiastes to remind us, "There is no new thing under the sun."

Which, apart from being a true thing, is actually a good thing. Because innovation is not about more new things. The new is not a product. It can never actually be a product. So what is innovation about?

I think Miranda can help us here: Innovation is about a sense of wonder based in a unique human experience that is brought to bear on the world-as-it-is. (I would argue, by the by, that wonder is not always a pleasant thing. Horror is a form of wonder and not less important or less truthful or less needful for being less pleasant.) We innovate as artists when we introduce our own experience of the world into the cultural conversation, when we honestly articulate our experience of the world to the world. The newness of an artistic innovation is in the uniqueness of the vision that produces it, not in its novelty. It's inevitable that whatever we create comes from our encounter with what other people have created. That's one of the great and beautiful things about being human: All that we are and all that we do comes from being in relationship with the world—with our time, our place, and with the people, things, cultures, ideas which make us the people we come to be. I truly believe that if we want to be innovative, all that's necessary is that we be true to those relationships that have created us, true to our encounter with the world.

No one is in any need of more new things that aren't actually new. But what makes life more interesting, what best reveals the mystery, wonder, complexity and horror of the human adventure, is a multiplicity and diversity of visions, of ways of thinking about the world. Innovation lies in the articulation of such visions. We owe it to ourselves and to future generations to create (to innovate!) lasting structures in which this multiplicity and diversity of visions can be fostered and supported.

How beauteous mankind is, indeed!

Mark Schultz is a playwright and seminarian. His plays include *The Blackest Shore*; *Ceremony*; *The Gingerbread House*; *Everything Will Be Different: A Brief History of Helen of Troy* (2005 Oppenheimer Award, 2006 Kesselring Prize). He is a member of New Dramatists and Rising Phoenix Rep.

ACT FIVE
LET'S

GEOGRAPHIES OF LANGUAGE: JOHN JESURUN

In an interview with Caridad Svich

CARIDAD SVICH: I think if you were to ask people on the street what they thought of when they heard the word "innovation," the response might be something along the lines of something to do with technology. So much, after all, of the technological progress in this, the digital age, has been in that area. I would hazard, that unless someone were thinking about 3D technology in film and CGI, motion-capture or other aspects of animation in film, the word "theatre" or "live performance" would rarely come up. But, of course, as practitioners in the field, we strive for excellence and personal, creative innovation, I hope, every day. When I first came upon your work, it was on the page. It was the play *White Water* in the TCG publication *On New Ground*. I never had seen anything quite like that play. I was smitten with it and baffled by it (on the page). In a good way. It haunted me. I was a grad student in theatre at the time. In my first year of grad school, and I had no idea what this beautiful text was, but I knew that it was different and that it knocked me off my seat and made me think about what was possible in theatre-making in a completely different way. The innovation for me was visible on the page in terms of structure and your use of language— the poetry of it and the possibilities the language offered to rethink everyday life.

Now I would guess that when most people think about your work, they think of your design—scenic/media—first. Perhaps before the poetry of your language. They think about the images and your manipulation of them. That's just a guess. But we live in a visual culture and often images do come first for folks. However, I can't help but think that even on the page without copious photographic accompaniment, your manipulation of language is what startles me and continues to wake me up as an artist. All to say: innovation with language. How we hear it in the theatre/performance. How we are conditioned to hear it. And how meaning and form shift before us as spectators of your work because of your use of language. Can you talk about this? In terms of the evolution of your work? Or projects in which you are currently involved?

JOHN JESURUN: I come from a bilingual family (Spanish/English) and early on I learned that language had the potential to be very fluid. For me this generated an endless interest in the mysterious origins of constructions, meanings and incongruous forms inside people's heads. The idea that thoughts could travel simultaneously in parallel but not symmetrical paths inspired a lot of possibilities. Not only about language but about kinds of space. I tend to think of forms in context to one another so ideas about one form get reflected into another form. For example, I can relate language to architecture in that it is a kind of construction full of support systems fused with design elements that hold it together. To me the difference with language is that the building doesn't always have to stay up. Conversations can be built and fall apart and altered and rebuilt again to great effect over time in a performance. The nature of logic, persuasion and emotion gives the geography of language its amazing layers and variety. Within these natural ups and downs we can trace bodies attempting to communicate through sound and space. They have ceased to become objects or flat images. Garbo speaks!

My own writing began very quickly out of necessity. I had to write a new episode and present it every week. It immediately set me to interrelate speed, economy and form to content. These demands opened up areas full of untapped content integrated with form. Quandaries like "form follows function," "the form IS the content" always interested me since art school. Because of this time and form restraint the most important ideas came to the forefront and the rest went on the back burner. I had to fill time and space with words. I was thinking specifically "film/video mediated time," which was different to me than live time. It was a more compacted way of deciphering content. I realized then that as forms, technology, society change, the content also begins to change to address it. These changes influenced my writing, its content and form. A lot of the early work looks like e-mail posts. There is a conversation of short sentences but you can't always tell who it's between. In some ways it was more about making contact than telling stories or exchanging content. It juxtaposed the idea of clarity with the rapidly increasing ubiquity and safety of the vague. One thing that was there was the constant collision of word/ideas as if the language was revolting against itself. Sections of the early work were usually punctuated by short monologues which over time have gotten longer and longer. I think what previously was spread out over many consecutive sentences has now merged into longer slower forms. Forms equally as considered but with a different sense of time. All this was developing as the technology integrated with it developed. My writing was greatly dependent on the talents of the actors and their ability to deal with the technology. Many of the more difficult texts I wrote were inspired by their willingness and ability to perform the challenge. Since the text, design and direction were formed together they always had an intimate relationship with each other. From the beginning, the fragility of the technology made me into a survivalist. Meaning that even if this technology broke we would still have the text and the speaker. So the text had to be able to survive on its own. My directive to the actors was: "If everything breaks, even if we are in complete darkness, as long as you keep talking we still have something."

As far as the content goes, early on we wouldn't find out what it really was about till halfway through the run. Not so much anymore but this was the excitement of discovering yourselves through your work. The content usually demands its own form. Part of the challenge is to get them to work together. Often the apparent "story" would parallel the actual stage and media setup. An example, *Deep Sleep* (1986) was "about" a struggle between mediated screen characters and live performers over who was real, who was trapped in whose world. Onstage the live actors conversed with the screen presences by speaking in the prescribed blank areas of the soundtrack. The screen actors and live performers were interlocked inside a mediated structure that stifled their identities.

SVICH: I want to chat a little bit about dreaming, and the value of quixotic dreams in the process of making art. This goes to also not looking for the end goal immediately/the "product"—which I think in at least U.S. culture is quite prevalent model for working—often "What is it?" "What is it about?" are the first questions asked of the work in order to fix it in place, but if you are interested in fluid meanings and fluidity itself as an artist, such questions may not even apply.

JESURUN: I do think the value of just making "work" has been devalued in search of a "product," complete and saleable, ready for the gallery, ready to eat. The message is that it should mean only one thing, rather than possess fluidity, that confuses people. Meaning we don't want to see any "artist marks" on it. It should look like definable, accessible work otherwise it has no "value" in the market. And that may be true for a certain kind of market. This removes the artist's fingerprint from his/her own work. It diminishes any real out-of-the-box searching. It makes it a different kind of artwork. There is work now that artists show each other that they would never show an art bureaucrat. I think this expectation of showing the "market" work removes the conversation between artists, each other and the audience. There's now kind of a private work and a more public work going on which is too bad. This reticence to reveal one's real direction is a mark of the conservative, cautious times. It's too bad to see such a lack of real instinct and fearlessness. It seems the stakes are high though with so much competition. It sounds like I'm talking about the business world doesn't it?

This makes me think of probably the dozens of rock songs I can listen to for years and I still have no idea what they "mean" but they do have a meaning. And they mean something to many people. But they aren't sitting around judging the value of the meaning. They are experiencing it. That these songs continue to resonate is a testament to the powerful, fearless intent in their creation. Luckily they will never be subject to stifling academic arbiters the way much "independent progressive" theater is nowadays. But I think that's because that music culture rejected those controls and was able to survive long enough to make some great work. Certainly with the help of some enlightened music companies of the time. Alas, I don't think the nonprofit industrial complex is half as enlightened as those apparently more commercial music producers were. They really believed in that work and the people that made it.

SVICH: What are you working on now? What new or old questions are you asking and demanding of the work and why?

JESURUN: Right now I'm working on several things. I'm in Japan researching the 17th century writer Saikaku Ihara for the second part of my last work *Stopped Bridge of Dreams*. Saikaku wrote many amazing stories about daily life at that time. I'm also working on my continuing web serial *Shadowland*. Part of it is written by me and part of it improvised by the actors. This is a very different way of working for me which I have found very enriching to the whole experience. Also, shooting and editing everything is a much more immediate and satisfying way of working for me right now than theater. We can cover a lot of ground and content in a very intimate way. There is no desperate need for narrative. It's film, video, poetry, Internet, so in that way it's a very liberating experience and has opened up the door to working with many new people and ideas. The form allows for fluidity and exactitude at the same time.

SVICH: Do you think of your poetry differently now than when you first started writing?

JESURUN: I think my writing has gone through different periods. It developed from short episodes to longer high-speed pieces full of urgency which would stop once in a while for a bit of poetry. There was a real period of "the fast and the furious" in the writing, which gradually slowed down some and became more poetic and intricate as far as use of words. Now it seems to be a mixture of both. With the work on my new serial it has opened it up to all of these things mixed with natural conversational tones and improvisation. Since the beginning I've tried to bring the world into the writing with multiple references to all kinds of history and culture. Now with the serial it has brought even more of the world into it in terms of content. The simultaneous combination of personal, social and political ideas for me is much more expansive with video. It puts even more demands on the writing I find. The camera and the editing are writing tools as well for me as they are in my stage work.

SVICH: How do you keep challenging yourself over the years?

JESURUN: For me, in terms of creativity, one show usually leads into another. Finishing one show always leaves questions and new challenges that need to be met. Making them happen is another question. Thankfully there is still an underground economy of artists that work beyond the marketplace. I think these artists keep each other going. You really have to go where the work is. I've been able to work a lot in other languages which greatly interests me. It has also expanded my work in many ways I hadn't imagined. Challenging ideas in our world are not only associated with technology. All kinds of innovations are happening without technology as the reason. In some ways technology has taken over for what is thought to be creativity. Forms are repeatedly tossed aside only to return again with a vengeance.

Remember when painting was "dead?" I think fluidity of connections between all these forms regardless of technology is important. If not you are just following the technology or technique when it should be following you.

John Jesurun—writer/director/media artist. Text, direction and design for thirty plus pieces including: the sixty-one-episode *Chang in a Void Moon*, the media trilogy *Deep Sleep/White Water/Black Maria*, *Philoktetes*, *FAUST/How I Rose* and *Firefall*. *Shatterhand Massacree and other Media Texts* is published by *Performing Arts Journal*. His work is also published by NoPassport Press, and has been seen at Soho Rep, Dance Theater Workshop and BAM. He also directed Jeff Buckley's video "Last Goodbye" and Harry Partch's opera *Delusion of the Fury* at Japan Society. His web serial *Shadowland* is on Vimeo.

WRITING AS GLOBAL ENGAGEMENT: AYAD AKHTAR

In an Interview with Caridad Svich

CARIDAD SVICH: You are not only a playwright, but also an actor, novelist and screenwriter. How do you, if at all, find yourself negotiating these related yet distinct creative identities?

AYAD AKHTAR: I think of myself as a dramatic storyteller, irrespective of the form. I think it's how my mind works, how I process the world, experience. Seeing things in movement, in a particular kind of movement native to the dramatic form: Movement through reversal to points of recognition. I think I've always been this way. Intcrested in opposition, in the movement between poles of possibility, in what changes when this kind of movement happens.

SVICH: Are they ever in conflict? For example, might an idea for a novel suddenly become a play when you would rather it would be a novel?

AKHTAR: Each idea seems to have some natural inclination. Some require more interiority, others less. Sometimes an idea seems to call for a kind of being with the characters that can only happen when actors incarnate people, and allow for the sort of carnal possibilities that arise, the fierce devotion—even love—that a portrayal can occasion. Other times, the imagination of the reader is best allowed to make what it will without this sort of concreteness. So far, there hasn't really been a conflict for me.

SVICH: Do you approach each form of writing—prose, drama and screenplay—differently? If so, how? In regard to innovation—the huge, encompassing topic of this salon—how do you seek the new? Push yourself and challenge yourself as an artist—via form, content or both?

AKHTAR: Inventiveness to me has to do with meeting the audience in a place of aliveness. Formal innovation can be the portal to that, but often formal innovation can actually be an impediment to the kind of directness I seek. I do think that having an awareness of the history of a form is important, but if you find yourself—as an artist—in dialogue with that history more than with the audience, then you might find yourself sacrificing something at the level of aliveness. Creative engagement with the world means not only engagement with the tradition, but with the world we are living in now. Brecht is kind of a paradigmatic figure for me in that regard, an artist who sought to speak to the world in which he was living, even if it meant that the work might not speak quite as powerfully to posterity as it did to those in his own time. I suspect someone like Beckett stands at something of the other extreme.

SVICH: When I work with younger writers, often the topic of whether to write a "universal" story invariably comes up. Sometimes there is this fear of being too "local," or too "culturally specific" because there is a misguided assumption that locality in writing, might, in turn, potentially alienate an audience. Of course, we know that theatre, to choose one medium for this conversation's purposes, is about transformation. I don't live in Shakespeare's Illyria or Mantua or Tennessee Williams's New Orleans or August Wilson's Pittsburgh, but when I witness the work, I enter the space metaphorically. All to say, have you ever wrestled as a writer with this very question of universality? And how have you gone through and past it conceptually and in practical terms in your works?

AKHTAR: Absolutely. It has been the central crossing of my writing career. I had a very formative experience in high school with a literature teacher who introduced me to writing. She had a passion for the great European modernist tradition, notably the writers of the French Existentialists and the Central European writers like Musil, Mann, Rilke and Kafka. I read so much of that stuff in my late teens, I means tons and tons of it. And I carried around a kind of assumption for years—without even realizing it—that writing in a universal way meant to me writing in a way that was specific to a particular tradition. Of course, that tradition—however wonderful—had very little to do with the specifics of my experience as a young Muslim-American in the Midwest. And so for the longest time, I had this feeling that I couldn't write about my own life. Or if I did, it would have to be in some veiled or elliptical way, with identity somehow erased or at the margins, pressing in. I wrote like that for ten years, and it didn't amount to much. It just didn't have life. I was trying too hard to be something I wasn't. Sometime in my early thirties, I realized what I was doing. And I realized that it wasn't just an issue in my writing, but in my psychic makeup. On some level, I was running from who I was. Once I started to realize this, everything changed. And not just on the level of content, but form as well. I had resisted the familiarity of movie narrative structure, of the immediacy of movies. After all, that was what I grew up on, film and TV. So as I started to write more about what was familiar to me, I began to gravitate more and more to telling stories in film-inspired form, whether I was writing a play or a novel or a movie.

Something I now see very clearly—and which writing teachers are always saying, but which I just had to figure out for myself—is that the concretely-felt particular is the best portal to the universal. It took me a very long time to understand just how true this is.

SVICH: Your play *The Invisible Hand* premiered at the Repertory Theatre of St. Louis in 2012 under Seth Gordon's direction. The play centers (for readers who may not be familiar with the play) on the plight of an investment banker being held for ransom in Pakistan by Islamic militants, and the complex and thorny relationship that develops between the kidnapped banker and his captor. While the play is structured, in part, along the familiar designs of a thriller, it actually becomes, as the 75 minutes of its run time play on, a lesson of sorts on international finance and an ambiguous morality play. In *Disgraced*, the posh dinner party—the rich who might and do behave badly—a trope audiences recognize quite well—turns into a fiery debate and exploration of radical Islam and terrorism—and matters of faith and identity. Might you speak to both plays and their dialectical structures?

AKHTAR: I am interested in engaging audiences as profoundly as I can. Which means engaging not only their emotions, but to engage them on the level of intellectual imagination, and also to meet them in the matters that have to do with their own lives. In *Disgraced*, I wanted to engage the audience's desire to be in that room, with a group of sexy people on the Upper East Side, living the life, talking about ideas. I wanted them to feel as I sometimes did when watching the Woody Allen films I loved so much in college, *Manhattan, Annie Hall, Hannah and Her Sisters*. I wanted to be one of those people. And this meant I invested so much more deeply in those stories. With *The Invisible*

Hand, there is a different kind of audience implication at work. The play is about finance, about the stock market, and I am fully aware that so much of the audience is personally invested in these matters. On a daily basis. Indeed, after the play was over, audience members would sometimes seek me out to ask me what stock tips I had, whether I thought they should sell Apple, etc. It meant that the play was making them think about their own 401k(s), about their personal finances, etc. Some of this was by design, an awareness on my part that writing this play a certain way meant it would draw viewers in more deeply. Audience engagement, that's what it's always about for me.

SVICH: And also too to the processes with both in the practice hall and production? Did conversations arise, for instance, with your respective artistic/creative teams about the politics of representation?

AKHTAR: There were lots of discussions around this with *Disgraced.* At the end of the day, though, while these discussions were helpful in getting actors understand more clearly what the play was about, these discussions were not necessarily creative in nature. More than anything, the discussions were about making everyone just a little more comfortable with something that wasn't very comfortable at all. It's a difficult play, and there isn't a simple discourse that can sit neatly atop it. In many ways, *Disgraced* is about the limits of discourse when it comes to race and identity, and so the trouble is never resolved. That's not always an easy place to leave an audience as an actor.

SVICH: Do you mean prejudices audiences may have walking into the work?

AKHTAR: Again, there were discussions about this, but they were not of material importance to the creative work.

One of the wonders of working with director Kimberly Senior on the play was that she understood how to keep the actors focused on the play itself, and not on what the play could be said to be saying, etc. I do understand the desire to feel that one is doing something responsible, but that is not—in my opinion—a matter of concern for the artist. This sort of focus on the optics of representation can be an impediment to the exploration of things-as-they-are. I don't think of art as an alternate universe that is intended to correct the dissonances of the world we are living in. If anything, art—as I see it—should thrust us more deeply, more humanly, more completely into those very dissonances. As such, *Disgraced* is resolutely not a corrective, not a public relations gesture intended, say, to humanize Muslims or some such for an audience that might be riddled with prejudices. Another way of saying it: Dialogue with the audience in the form of a simple dialectic intended to oppose their prejudices is perhaps an admirable goal, but I don't see it as an artistic one.

SVICH: Are there any discomforts actors may have in playing the flawed natures of your characters—particularly Amir Kapoor in *Disgraced*?

AKHTAR: As I've addressed this to some degree above, let me just comment on the matter of flawed characters. I see drama as the result of our flawed natures, as an inquiry into those flawed natures. Our flawed natures are the entire subject of drama. Without flawed characters, there are no stories. No life in the work, no sense of recognition or reality in the work, no vitality, and above all, no audience engagement. As you can tell, I feel pretty strongly about this!

SVICH: You majored in theater at Brown University and then studied acting with Grotowski abroad for a year. How did training with Grotowski shape you as not only an actor but as a writer? How has it affected your process of art-making?

AKHTAR: Working with Grotowski was this single most formative experience of my early adulthood. But it wasn't the "Grotowski form" that so affected me. His aesthetic was deeply informed by his Eastern European sensibility and had very little resonance for me artistically. It was his example. The singularity of his uncompromising vision, the way in which he had so fully shaped his life to his calling. He had a peerless intellect, a wide-ranging understanding not only of the theater, but of the human, and all of this was married to a staggering capacity to sit in the questions, not reaching for answers. Keats called this capacity "negative capability." G had it in spades, and being exposed to it fundamentally affected not only what it meant to me to be an artist, but affected my understanding of what was possible as an artist.

SVICH: Many of the contributors to this collection have expressed to me the difficulties of making work that is or may be classified as "innovative" within the larger scope of an industry that may place its market values elsewhere. How sometimes, oftentimes, the very question of value—what is granted value culturally vis-à-vis box office returns and so forth—can confuse the issue itself of innovation, and indeed—and this is the term I prefer—the making of visionary work. Do you see the role of the market and the role of the cultural work we do as artists as in or out of sync? And in what ways do you think actionable steps can be taken towards a more sustainable arts culture within the wider culture of society and politics?

AKHTAR: I have a particular point of view on this matter that is, perhaps, unusual. I spent a bunch of years making a living writing screenplays, and I learned a lot from it. I learned from the traditional forms. I learned from the demand of making the work engaging page to page. I learned from the pressures of the audience, the market, the producer. In film, if you can't make a scene work, you get fired. And "making a scene work" is not something that you define. Others are defining it for you. Of course, that orientation has its dangers, but it bears noting that there can be much to learn from approaching work this way as well. I have sometimes felt that in the American theater, the writer is accorded too much authority. It doesn't always foster an environment where engaging the audience is as important as it should be.

SVICH: Some of my colleagues feel that perhaps, after some time in U.S. theatre where work being made looked inward—toward domestic concerns and so forth—that theatre makers are starting to look outward again—to make work with a global lean/perspective, to position their making and thinking about work outside of narrow definitions of identity, nationhood and such. What responsibilities do you think we have as artists to keeping the global and local in dialogue, dialectical or not, in our art-making? And how can we educate our audiences to think beyond the "kitchen sink?"

AKHTAR: Again, to me it isn't really a question of responsibility. Other than the responsibility to do good work. That's what is going to get people thinking and feeling. I think the danger with the narrower frame, the proverbial kitchen sink, is that it does seem to foster an idea of art as a kind of expression of what we already know. Art as self-expression, as it were. I like to think of art in a different light, as a process of engagement, a creative involvement with the world. Pushing beyond the known is part of that process, I believe.

Ayad Ahktar is an actor and writer. His plays include *Disgraced*, which received the 2013 Pulitzer Prize in Drama and the 2013 OBIE Award, *The Invisible Hand* and *The Who and the What*. His works have been staged across the United States and abroad. His novel *American Dervish* was published in 2012.

A BOOK GROUP FOR THEATRE

Maddy Costa

You saw the show—
the one with the rave reviews and the star ratings strung up like fairy
lights;
or the one in the warehouse across town that you were scared to attend;
the one with big themes: race, war, the degradations of inequality;
or the one so naked you could hardly bear to watch.

You saw the show—
but now what?

Is there someone to talk to about what this show made you think,
how it made you feel,
not just in the hour after but
a week later
a fortnight later?

Is there a forum for discussion, something
other than the traditional post-show, in which those
voices of authority and expertise—

you know,
the playwright, the director, the actor,
the critic—

share their interpretations
without space being made to explore yours?

And if the answer is no,
is that OK?

And if the answer is no,
to what extent does this limit theatre's collaboration with its audience?

And if the answer is no,
what happens to the hope at the end of the evening?

That last line, *what happens to the hope at the end of the evening*, is the title of a show I saw twice in 2013, a show that thinks out loud about community, friendship bonds and the potentially radical act of going to the theatre. It posits theatre as an inherently hopeful act, in which people gather to "see where we are [and] think about where we might be going." The narrator, Andy—played by the show's co-author, Andy Smith—is studying for a Ph.D. in "what the theatre does, and what it might be able to do." Partway through, he shares a fragment of his research:

"In her 2009 book *Theatre & Audience*, Helen Freshwater writes the following: 'Our sense of the proper, or ideal relationship between theatre and its audiences can illuminate our hopes for other models of social interaction.' She suggests that the theatre is a place in which we can clarify thought around some of our expectations of community, of democracy, of citizenship."

As someone who doesn't make, but thinks, talks and writes about theatre—a critic, but a stretchy and unconventional interpretation of that word—I'm also interested in forging new models of social interaction. Finding new ways for people who make, watch and write about theatre not simply to inhabit a space together but to talk with each other, to share. This is the manifesto of Dialogue, the "collaborative playspace" I curate with my friend Jake Orr (founder and artistic director of British organization A Younger Theatre). As Dialogue, Jake and I have taken residence within theatres and festivals, experimented with "embedded criticism" and advocated for local critical communities. But our most consistent and successful activity is our Theatre Club: informal discussion events modeled on the book group, in which a motley community of people gather to discuss a specific show.

These are the thoughts around my expectations of community, of democracy, of citizenship, that Dialogue Theatre Club clarifies and puts into practice:

There are no voices of authority.
(No one involved in the show under discussion is present.)

One opinion is as valid as another,

one interpretation is as valid as another.
We are attentive to each other's voices
respectful and responsive.

We are talking about theatre, but through that so much more:
politics
equality
race
gender
history
education
humanity.

We judge neither the show nor each other.

We look through each other's eyes
and see the show anew.

I wish Jake and I could claim the idea as our own, but that credit goes to Lily Einhorn, the remarkable manager of the Two Boroughs participation project at the Young Vic Theatre in London. In a blog describing the thinking behind the Two Boroughs Theatre Club that she established in 2012, with me as host, Lily writes:

"A lack of language—not of basic understanding of English, but theatrical and artistic language—is not something we regularly, or readily, address in participation. How do you discuss what you have seen if you do not have the words? Or anyone to use those words with?"

Here are some things people who attend the Two Boroughs or Dialogue Theatre Clubs discover:

You don't need access to a specialist language to talk about theatre.

You don't need to know the history of a text or its performance;
you don't need to be au fait with avant-garde trends;
you don't even need to know upstage from downstage
(I don't).

It's just a conversation. People talking

about what they saw and heard
on a stage,
or in a performance space,

what it made them think,
why it made them feel.

What they understood
and what left them confused.

If you don't want to talk,
that's fine, too.
Hearing is as important as being heard.

In the democratic, communal spaces created by the Theatre Club,
I'm no longer The Critic: I'm simply another member of the audience.
Others at the Club might work in theatre, but they're just as likely to be
lawyers, charity workers, teachers, communications officers, parents,
unemployed. At one Dialogue Theatre Club, a woman who works in
child protection shared her views alongside a bus driver. At another,
a puppeteer chatted with medical students specializing in mental
health. Sometimes we will gather directly post-show, but more often—
and more successfully—we see the show on different nights; unlike in
conventional criticism, which fixes theatre in the glare of the press
night, Theatre Club appreciates the process and multiplicity of live
performance that is recreated night after night. Whenever Theatre Club
takes place, we always aim to have drinks and food (wine, juice, crisps,
biscuits) in the room. How better to make people feel comfortable than
by providing home comforts?

Since beginning to host Theatre Clubs in 2012, I have had a number
of gratifying conversations with participants. The theme is usually the
same: I don't have anyone else to talk to about theatre; I've always been
too scared to talk about theatre, in case people thought I was stupid; I
didn't understand or enjoy the show but after this conversation I'd like
to see it again. This feeling of transformation is reciprocal: my sense
of the kind of critic I want to be, and the conversations I want theatre
to open up for me, has changed radically. And seeing theatre through
the eyes of people for whom it's not a profession but an enthusiasm
or even less, an occasional entertainment, an object of mild curiosity,

has enriched my appreciation incalculably more than a lifetime spent reading reviews.

Because theatre—
the theatre I believe in and want to see—
isn't about how much you know.

It's not about privileged information, or specialist education.

It's some people, in a room, telling a story
or sharing a way of looking at the world.

It's a place where strangers can congregate
without suspicion
or competition
or hostility.

A place of hope.

Theatre Clubs thrive because they are this place, too.

Maddy Costa is a writer, crafter, dreamer and mother of two, based in London. A theatre and music critic since 1998, she writes for the *Guardian* and *Exeunt,* is critic-in-residence with Chris Goode & Company, and collaborates with Dialogue and Something Other to stretch what critical practice might be.

LET'S

Julie Felise Dubiner

So much has changed in the 20 years or so since I was the Associate Director of Ticket Services at a big regional (gosh, I have had some great titles to make up for crappy paychecks). For sure, the way we spend our spare time and spare change is markedly different. So are the ways we create plays. But the systems we put in place back at the dawn of the regional theater movement and the heyday of the subscriber years remain. We build on top of them, trying to squeeze them into a modern reality. It's time to tear some things down. Are we just stuck in a loop of protecting and preserving institutions instead of revitalizing and preparing for the future?

Let's make new mistakes.

What would happen if every theater held a TBA slot when they started their season? I proposed this idea at the 21st Century Literary Office convening in 2012. A major artistic director loudly snorted. Like, loudly. Like, I stopped and looked around loudly. In the manifesto (*http:// howlround.com/i-dare-us-a-manifesto-on-the-21st-century-literary- office*), I went on to suggest that we get rid of seasons all together. The subscription model no longer serves the artists or the audiences, so why do we cling to it? If we could switch up show times, perhaps we'd be more available to potential audiences, and if we could chuck our calendars and start over, we would be able to be more nimble, especially in the production of new work. We have crammed every play and musical into the same rehearsal slots, our design deadlines get earlier and earlier, and we have no room to add previews or continue working. Sure, we apply for grants to pay for more rehearsal time, but the systems keep us from truly bending time to our will. I swear, if I hear one more freighter ship metaphor invoked by management about why change never comes, I'm gonna scream and cry. Aw, hell. I already scream and cry. If we start with a TBA slot, we could begin to untangle what our production departments need, respond to our audiences and program shows with immediate relevancy, and focus more on the production of plays rather than the development of scripts.

I fear, or feel, that I and my fellow practitioners of professional dramaturgy have been complicit in creating barriers and enabled our leaders to maintain an outdated status quo. It is time to eliminate the titles of literary manager and dramaturg. "Dramaturg" in particular is a useless and opaque word, and does not represent the kind of leaders we thought we were training to be. We contribute to the problem of bloated administrative staffs and ridiculously long development processes, while not having the time, resources, or power to develop real relationships with artists in our role as resident and their role as visitor. To be clear, all staff members should be dramaturgs. Our leadership should be thinking dramaturgically and bringing dramaturgs in as leaders. We must all ask good questions, but somewhere along the line, the dramaturg was no longer expected to have answers or original thoughts. No one snorted when I proposed this, but I was depressed for weeks that we didn't get into any meaningful conversations about anything. And super-depressed that a colleague I greatly respect actually said she had tried everything at her theater and there is no better way. I didn't snort, or scream, or cry. I sat there stunned, and left wanting nothing to do with the dramaturgs and literary managers who don't want to lead, reinvent and change.

I still hear that A.D.'s snort. And I am haunted by the lack of critical dialogue among my group of supposedly critical thinkers. I don't know if these ideas would change anything, but as collaborators, how dare we snort when someone has an idea? Argue, build on the idea, or have an even better idea. Just have an idea.

To be sure, some dramaturgs and their colleagues are evaluating, innovating and developing relationships with their audiences beyond newsletters and post-show discussions, and a new-play database is being built. My pride for the program I work on, American Revolutions at Oregon Shakespeare Festival, knows no bounds. It is amazing to be part of this project where we work so hard to use our resources to empower the artists. We trust them to drive the timetable and development process for their commissions. And, yet we still, all of us, struggle to do good work for good audiences in an over-scheduled, inflexible and outdated world.

Thomas Paine said, "We have it in our power to begin the world again." Let us begin. Let us argue, build and think. Let's.

Julie Felise Dubiner is the Associate Director of American Revolutions: the United States History Cycle at the Oregon Shakespeare Festival. From 2004–2010, Julie was the Resident Dramaturg at Actors Theatre of Louisville. Prior to Louisville, she was in Philadelphia as Project Manager of the Rosenbach Company and Dramaturg at Prince Music Theater. Julie holds degrees from Tufts and Columbia.

WHO GETS TO PLAY?
(AN EPILOGUE)

August Schulenburg

An epilogue after five acts? While our age of deficient attentions might deem that gilding an overlong lily, one of our greatest innovators, William Shakespeare, knew better. After five acts in the dark possibilities of a theatre, an epilogue is often required to survive the transition into the lights-up of life. Like deep-sea divers returned to the surface, or astronauts come home from space, our bodies need time to adjust to the shifting pressures of fantasy into reality.

But I am no Puck, here to tell you that the forty visions of this volume are merely shadows. The forty theatre-makers and their contentious dialogues barely contained within these pages are after something more than dreams. Each in their own unique way is asking more from us: from you, dear reader; from me, the writer attempting this old-fashioned epilogue; and from all of us with the guts and gumption to claim that this art form older than agriculture still matters in a digital age.

How shall we answer them?

First, a digression by way of gratitude: we owe an enormous note of thanks for the indefatigable energies of the editor of this book and online curator of the blog salon that seeded it, Caridad Svich. When TCG originally asked her to curate a salon of essays along the themes of our 2013 National Conference, I assumed she'd turn in somewhere between 10 to 15 posts. I was the happiest kind of wrong about that! This volume is only part of the tremendous abundance of passion and thought she brought back, and I encourage you to read all the essays on the TCG Circle: *http://www.tcgcircle.org*. That such abundance came from one of our most prolific playwrights is all the more remarkable. Caridad, thank you.

As a second digression, it's worth noting that this book itself represents an innovation of sorts. TCG has first and foremost been a publisher of playwrights, committing to our authors over their careers (and garnering 14 Pulitzer Prize-winning plays along the way). This inaugural Sourcebook represents the first time we've published content that emerges directly from our programming—in this case, our 2013 and 2014 National Conferences—and also our first title to live primarily as an eBook. Whether or not this inaugural Sourcebook becomes the first of many or the last of its kind remains to be seen, but either way, it represents an innovative step in the journey of TCG Books.

My digressions now are ended, and we return again to this question of what exactly an epilogue to 40 variations of innovation should be. I have both an institutional and individual answer, and I'll begin, as a good employee should, with the institution.

TCG is now several years into a strategic plan in three parts: the Equity, Diversity & Inclusion Initiative; the Audience (R)Evolution program; and our Theatre Nation project. I could fill what little word count I have describing all the exciting pieces of these parts, but what's important to our epilogue is a discovery that we've only recently made. What had seemed at first to be three equally important yet distinct parts now stand revealed as different aspects of a single question; a question which weaves itself throughout each of these forty essays, sometimes subtly, and at other times, with a brazen urgency:

Who gets to play?

Our Equity, Diversity & Inclusion Initiative seeks to dismantle barriers to opportunities in our field, creating a more diverse and equitable answer to the question, who gets to play?

Our Audience (R)Evolution program champions audience engagement and community development models that, in many cases, radically re-imagine the answer to the question, who gets to play?

And our Theatre Nation project explores new ways for TCG to engage our field beyond the formal structures of membership, because it's not just a question of who gets to play, but also, who will write the rules of the game?

With its diversity of voices, this book represents one answer, with forty theatre-makers—and many more represented on the Circle—engaging with the conversations of the Conference, regardless of whether or not they could attend.

That's my institutional response. My personal answer cannot help but emerge from my status as a new father of a nine month-old daughter. Now, there may be nothing particularly innovative about having a baby. After all, it's the oldest change in the book.

Yet nothing makes me feel the dizzying possibilities of life like watching her bump up against the world. Everything is new. Anything is possible. And isn't that what the rare bird of truly great theatre makes us feel?

All these innovations, from green theatre to transmedia, from site-specific to community-based, all of them are in service of something very old. It is the force that drives my daughter to reach over all obstacles and, to her delight, grab something unexpected. It is the rush of everything is new, and anything is possible. It is life, that most merciless and magical of innovators. And when, through all the innovative means we can muster, we at last answer the question of who gets to play? with everyone, we will have a theatre worthy of passing on to our children.

The epilogue is over. The lights rise. What innovation, great or small, will you bring to the world today?

August Schulenburg is the Associate Director of Communications at Theatre Communications Group, the co-board chair of the Network of Ensemble Theaters, a Creative Partner of Flux Theatre Ensemble and a Playwrights Workshop Fellow at The Lark. He is an ensemble artist, actor, playwright, director, activist and new father, and you can learn more about him here: *https://augustschulenburg.wordpress.com*

AMERICAN THEATRE MAGAZINE

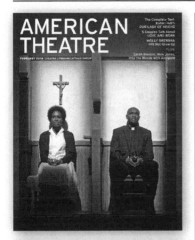

Become an INDIVIDUAL MEMBER of Theatre Communications Group, the national organization for the American theatre, and receive a **FREE** subscription to **AMERICAN THEATRE** magazine.

Receive 10 issues a year—including **5 complete new playscripts**—with an emphasis on presenting artists' voices, covering the diversity of the theatrical landscape and meeting the changing needs of a larger and more varied readership of our fast-evolving national and world theatre scene.

ADDITIONAL MEMBER BENEFITS INCLUDE:

UNLIMITED ACCESS to AmericanTheatre.org, including breaking news, stunning photos, exclusive videos and more!

20% DISCOUNT on resource materials, Including **ARTSEARCH®**

15% DISCOUNT on all books from TCG and other select theatre publishers including works by Annie Baker, Eric Bogosian, Caryl Churchill, David Henry Hwang, Tony Kushner, Suzan-Lori Parks, Sarah Ruhl, John Patrick Shanley, Paula Vogel and August Wilson.

DISCOUNTS on tickets at theatres across the country.

Receive the *Individual Member Wire*, TCG's bimonthly e-mail newsletter.

FREE membership with the Performing Arts Alliance.

We invite you to join us today and receive all of TCG's MEMBER BENEFITS!

Call TCG Customer Service at (212) 609-5900 or join online at www.tcg.org

For over 50 years, **Theatre Communications Group (TCG),**
the national organization for the American theatre, has existed
to strengthen, nurture and promote the professional not-for-profit
American theatre. TCG's constituency has grown from a handful
of groundbreaking theatres to nearly 700 member theatres and
affiliate organizations and more than 12,000 individuals nationwide.
TCG offers its members networking and knowledge-building
opportunities through conferences, events, research and communications;
awards grants, approximately $2 million per year, to theatre companies
and individual artists; advocates on the federal level; and serves as
the U.S. Center of the International Theatre Institute, connecting its
constituents to the global theatre community. TCG is North America's
largest independent publisher of dramatic literature, with 14 Pulitzer Prizes
for Best Play on the TCG booklist. It also publishes the award-winning
AMERICAN THEATRE magazine and ARTSEARCH®, the essential source
for a career in the arts. In all of its endeavors, TCG seeks to increase
the organizational efficiency of its member theatres, cultivate and
celebrate the artistic talent and achievements of the field and promote
a larger public understanding of, and appreciation for, the theatre.
For more information, visit **www.tcg.org.**